Praise for *Why Teach?*

"*Why Teach?* is a heartfelt and provocative book that will interest anyone who wonders what happened to the idea that college should be a life-altering, mind-expanding experience. With wry humor and hard-won wisdom, Mark Edmundson offers an inspiring vision of the liberal arts as a vehicle for personal transformation." **—Tom Perotta, author of**
Little Children* and *The Leftovers

"[A] deeply felt collection of explorations and reflections on an education in the liberal arts." **—*Kirkus Reviews***

"Mark Edmundson obviously missed the intellectual timidity gene that's so helpful for an academic career. He has the audacity to argue in this book that universities should not be business and consumer training facilities, internet hookup spots, and workout centers, but places where students grapple with 'perspective-altering' intellectual challenges."
—Gerald Graff, professor of English and education, University of Illinois at Chicago, former president, Modern Language Association

"[A] provocative tome." **—*New York Journal of Books***

"You may not like everything Mark Edmundson has to say in this shimmering series of essays, but you will never again need to ask his question, 'Why Teach?' Read his answers and make your own revolution." **—Megan Marshall, author of**
Margaret Fuller: A New American Life

WHY TEACH?

*The Fine Wisdom and Perfect Teachings of
the Kings of Rock and Roll: A Memoir*
The Death of Sigmund Freud: The Legacy of His Last Days
Why Read?
Teacher: The One Who Made the Difference
*Nightmare on Main Street: Angels, Sado-Masochism,
and the Culture of Gothic*
Literature Against Philosophy, Plato to Derrida: A Defence of Poetry
Wild Orchids and Trotsky: Messages from American Universities (ed.)
*Towards Reading Freud: Self-Creation in Milton, Wordsworth,
Emerson, and Sigmund Freud*

WHY TEACH?

In Defense of a Real Education

Mark Edmundson

BLOOMSBURY

NEW YORK · LONDON · OXFORD · NEW DELHI · SYDNEY

Bloomsbury USA
An imprint of Bloomsbury Publishing Plc

1385 Broadway	50 Bedford Square
New York	London
NY 10018	WC1B 3DP
USA	UK

www.bloomsbury.com

BLOOMSBURY and the Diana logo are trademarks of Bloomsbury Publishing Plc

First published 2013
This paperback edition published 2014

The following pieces previously appeared:
"Liberal Arts & Lite Entertainment" in *Harper's Magazine*; "Dwelling in Possibilities" in the *Chronicle of Higher Education*; "Who Are You and What Are You Doing Here? A Word to the Incoming Class" in *Oxford American*; "Do Sports Build Character?" in the *Chronicle of Higher Education*; "The Globalists" in the *Chronicle of Higher Education*; "My First Intellectual" on the *Chronicle of Higher Education*'s "Lingua Franca" blog; "The Pink Floyd Night School" in the *New York Times*; "A Word to the Incoming Humanities Professor" in *Hedgehog Review*; "Against Readings" in the *Chronicle of Higher Education*; "Narcissus Regards His Book/The Common Reader Now" in the *Chronicle of Higher Education*; "The Uncoolness of Good Teachers" in the *New York Times Magazine*; "Teaching the Truths" in *Raritan*; "Under the Sign of Satan: Blake in the Corporate University" in *Hedgehog Review*.

ISBN: HB: 978-1-62040-107-1
        PB: 978-1-62040-642-7
        ePub: 978-1-62040-108-8

Library of Congress Cataloging-in-Publication Data

Edmundson, Mark, 1952-
Why teach? : in defense of a real education / Mark Edmundson.
pages cm
ISBN 978-1-62040-107-1
1. Education, Higher— United States— Aims and objectives. I. Title.
LA227.4.E36 2013
378.73—dc23
2013000853

2 4 6 8 10 9 7 5 3

Typeset by Westchester Book Group
Printed and bound in the U.S.A. by Berryville Graphics Inc., Berryville, Virginia

To find out more about our authors and books visit www.bloomsbury.com. Here you will find extracts, author interviews, details of forthcoming events, and the option to sign up for our newsletters.

Bloomsbury books may be purchased for business or promotional use. For information on bulk purchases please contact Macmillan Corporate and Premium Sales Department at specialmarkets@macmillan.com.

Contents

CONTENTS

Introduction

Midway through the last decade of the twentieth century, American higher education changed. Colleges and universities entered a new phase in which they stopped being intellectually driven and culturally oriented and began to model themselves on businesses. They sought profit; they sought prestige: the more the better. To be sure, there had always been a commercial side to American higher education. But in the mid-nineties, universities began dropping pretenses and putting profit ahead of intellectual and (dare one say it?) spiritual values. This book reports on the change and attempts to combat it.

What does it mean for a university to stop seeing itself as having something like a spiritual mission and begin acting like a commercial venture? Many things: The shift the universities underwent was complex and had multiple dimensions. There were major technological changes, changes in the intellectual climate. As this book unfolds, it will offer a comprehensive picture. But we might begin by saying that at the center of it all was a shift in the role of students. Before 1995 or so, students had about as much say in the shaping of the university as members of a fairly well established religious community have in determining its moral codes and forms of worship. Which is to say, they had almost none. The professors ran the show: What was important to them was what mattered.

But things changed. Starting in 1960, the American birthrate began to decline. In 1974, it hit its lowest point in sixty years. The baby boom was emphatically over. Twenty years later, the kids born in the seventies were ready for college, but there simply weren't enough of them to supply the schools that had so happily expanded to accommodate the baby boom population.

The university of the early nineteen nineties was still geared to the enormous swell of kids born after the Second World War. When that previous population finally made its way through— like a juicy meal passing the length of a boa constrictor—the schools began to see trouble. How were they going to complete the freshman class? How were they going to pay for all the tenured professors and the entrenched deans brought on to educate the prior generation? Colleges can expand readily enough—hire more professors, hire more administrators, build more buildings. But with tenure locking professors in for lifelong employment, how do you get rid of surplus faculty when the market declines? What do you do with the dorms that threaten to stand empty? How do you fill all those potentially vacant seats in Psych 101?

The answer was obvious. The universities were going to have to pursue students much as businesses pursue customers. They were going to have to treat their prospective students as potential buyers. And they were going to have to treat their existing students as customers too, for students can always switch brands: They can always up and transfer. So securing customers and getting them to maintain brand loyalty became the order of the day. "Most colleges don't have admissions offices anymore," a college administrator told me in 1993. "They have marketing departments." Even those schools that had more applicants than places in the first-year class had to market aggressively. They were competing for prestige and position with other schools of their caliber. They were also competing for full-tuition payers. Everyone wanted the kids who weren't going to petition them for a full ride or nag for discounts come tuition time. Ultimately, too, the schools were competing for future money: The best students tend to become successful, and then (with luck) committed donors. "The primary purpose of Yale University," a Yale faculty member said not long ago, "is the production of wealthy alumni to further enrich Yale University."

How did the students respond to being treated like customers? They didn't seem to mind at all. From what one could see, they loved it. They were long accustomed to the consumer role. From the time that they were toddlers they'd been the targets of ads and ads and more ads. They were used to being addressed in the teasing, whimsical, and ultimately sycophantic advertising mode that the universities now felt compelled to use. The kids apparently adored being fawned on: They'd grown up in front of the television, being treated like monarchs of the marketplace. When the universities followed suit and began to address them with similar deference, the kids ate it up. On came expensive student centers, lavish gyms, gourmet dining, and slews of student service workers, deans and deanlets to cater to the whims of the customers. Universities began to look like retirement spreads for the young.

No surprise that when the kids got to the classroom they

demanded a soft ride: They wanted easy grading, lots of pass-fail courses, light homework, more laughs. If the professors didn't oblige, the kids flayed them on the course evaluations. Those evaluations had an impact on tenure, promotion, salary, and prestige. By and large, the professors caved.

In the old days, when the university was a quasi-churchly institution, the professors largely called the shots. (The ecclesiastical style of architecture at Yale and Duke and numberless other schools makes the old religious affiliations clear.) The professors disseminated scientific knowledge that could improve daily life and help us to understand nature. They promulgated literary and philosophic wisdom that initiated young people into the complexities of the adult world.

But in the new university all this changed. Now the professors were the people who gave the grades, period. They needed to be humored at all times and hearkened to occasionally. But anyone who revered them for their wisdom or wanted to emulate them was tacitly understood to be half-cracked. The word *professor* intoned in a certain way began to mean "learned fool."

As the professors' influence receded, the world of consumerism and entertainment enhanced its powers. In the mid-nineties, the kids were socialized into the consumer mentality by their new, two-hundred-station TV sets (and of course by their parents). The first chapter of this book, "On the Uses of the Liberal Arts," describes the confrontation between the TV-driven consumer ethos that the kids brought with them from home and the intellectual ethos of the university. At the time, many commentators ascribed the decline in American higher education to the advent of programmatically debunking cultural theory. Freud, Marx, and Derrida were at the root of all evil. If debunking theory did have an effect, it was largely because of how well it rhymed with the attitude of dismissive superiority that TV and commercial culture overall tended to stimulate.

Ten years later, in the middle of the new millennium's first decade, things changed again. Now kids weren't only being shaped by the belch-and-buy spirit of TV, but by the hurry-up consumer ethos of the Internet, which they patrolled with unsleeping vigilance. (We create our tools, Marshall McLuhan famously said, and then our tools create us.) To put it crudely: The students had been sped up. Now they were consuming, watching, enjoying, buying at a hyper-accelerated pace—living in overdrive. What they couldn't do was slow down: slow down to observe and examine, slow down to think. The second chapter, "Dwelling in Possibilities," tells how the new computer technology administered an adrenaline shot to the already robust rebellion against real education. Now the consumer worldview was more confident, further insinuated, tougher to budge. What was actually a product of culture—the buy-buy, do-do ethos—was beginning to feel more like a precipitate of human nature. And fighting what people believe to be natural is never an easy thing.

This book tries. It's addressed not to presidents and deans and boards of directors and trustees; it's not addressed to the chair of the faculty senate or to the consortium of student leaders. Most of these people are by now part of the problem. The book is addressed to individual teachers and most of all to students and their parents. It puts a diagnosis on the table and then offers strategies for dealing with it. In these pages I talk about how to get yourself a good education at an American college or university, even when the forces of the school itself are arrayed against you. (The major enemy of education in America now is American education, university education in particular.) There are astonishing opportunities to be had at almost all American colleges, and this book aims to inspire students to seek them out. I also want to offer teachers some resources to fight against the current modes of dull conformity that afflict us.

For education now is not for the individual. It is not geared to help him grow to his potential and let him find out what he truly loves and how he might pursue it. No. Education now is a function of society. This is the theme of the first section of the book, "The Shift." Current schooling, from the primary grades through college, is about tooling people to do what society (as its least imaginative members conceive it) needs done. We are educated to fill roles, not to expand our minds and deepen our hearts. We are tooled to slide into a social machine and function smoothly with a little application from time to time of the right pleasing grease. Education now prepares us for a life of conformity and workplace tedium, in exchange for which we can have our iPhones, our flat screens, our favorite tunes, Facebook, and Twitter. But what we want is real learning—learning that will help us see the world anew and show us that there could be more to our lives than we had thought.

Conservative jeremiads against the university tend to declare that universities are not doing their socializing job comprehensively enough. They want higher education to feed the demands of the American economy overall and of private enterprise in particular. The authors of such tracts are inclined to feel that one idea subversive of the status quo is one too many. In my view, universities are still functioning far too much in the service of conformity. Whether the academic idiom in play is conservative or purportedly radical—traditional or post-poststructuralist—schools now educate the mind and not the heart. The curriculum has become arid and abstract: Preprofessionalism is the order of the day. What Keats memorably called "Soul-making" is absent from current higher education. It needs to be restored.

How do you educate yourself, or, if you're a teacher, how do you try to educate others? The next section of the book is called "Fellow Students," for I think of myself as being a student of my discipline, as all teachers must be. In "Fellow Students," I talk to people who are still in school and trying to get themselves an education despite the odds. I offer plenty of advice: about how to read, about how to deal with professors, about how to struggle against a decadent university culture. I talk about the kind of education you can find in a classroom at its best, which is epitomized for me by what my great teacher Doug Meyers offered. I ask young people to ponder the virtues of failure and to think about what they can gain educationally from sports—and what they can lose. I reflect on what's called global education and I let students know why I think they should all—and I mean all—at least consider becoming English majors.

The final section of the book is called "Fellow Teachers," and it's addressed to my comrades in what can often seem like one of the impossible professions. I encourage people who teach in universities—and especially in humanities departments—to stop thinking of themselves as creators of so-called new knowledge (or "fresh paradigms," as the current jargon has it) and start thinking of themselves as teachers. I'd like them to imagine themselves as potential liberators, not only of the students in their classes but of the people outside of school who might attend their lectures or read what they write. I urge them to stop the professional posturing and prestige chasing and liberate themselves and others into the fields of joy and salutary change that the liberal arts at their best provide. I'd like them to step up and oppose the commercialization of their universities. I'd like them to think less about their careers and more about the hopes that brought them to the study of great books to begin with. I'd like some of them to cut the shit. I'd like all of us to have a little more fun.

I'd like us to blow a hole through the university's ethos of entertainment and training for success and to bury its wearisome work-hard, play-hard frat-boy ideology. We should blast away the customer-coddling deans and student service hacks; blast past academic pretension and the hunger for "standing in the field." Blast university presidents so afraid of offending a potential donor that they won't raise a word in behalf of social justice or political sanity. Blow away the trustees who think that they're a corporate board of directors and will not rest until their schools resemble Walmarts. Blast them all. And while you're doing it, have a good time. Because knowledge is joy. Creativity is ultimate freedom. Real thought is bliss. *Sapere aude,* as the old thinkers liked to say: Dare to Know; Dare to Be Wise!

THE SHIFT

LIBERAL ARTS & LITE
ENTERTAINMENT (1997)

TODAY IS EVALUATION day in my Freud class, and everything has changed. The class meets twice a week, late in
the afternoon, and the clientele, about fifty undergraduates,
tends to drag in and slump, looking disconsolate and a little lost,
waiting for a jump-start. To get the discussion moving, they
usually require a joke, an anecdote, an off-the-wall question—
When you were a kid, were your Halloween getups ego costumes, id costumes, or superego costumes? That sort of thing.
But today, as soon as I flourish the evaluation forms, a buzz rises
in the room. Today they write their assessments of the course,
their assessments of *me*, and they are without a doubt wide
awake. "What is your evaluation of the instructor?" asks question number eight, entreating them to circle a number between
5 (excellent) and 1 (poor, poor). Whatever interpretive subtlety
they've acquired during the term is now out the window. Edmundson: 1 to 5, stand and shoot.

And they do. As I retreat through the door—I never stay
around for this phase of the ritual—I look over my shoulder and
see them toiling away like the devil's auditors. They're pitched

into high writing gear, even the ones who struggle to squeeze out their journal entries word by word, stoked on a procedure they have by now supremely mastered. They're playing the informed consumer, letting the provider know where he's come through and where he's not quite up to snuff.

But why am I so distressed, bolting like a refugee out of my own classroom, where I usually hold easy sway? Chances are the evaluations will be much like what they've been in the past—they'll be just fine. It's likely that I'll be commended for being "interesting" (and I am commended, many times over), that I'll be cited for my relaxed and tolerant ways (that happens, too), that my sense of humor and capacity to connect the arcana of the subject matter with current culture will come in for some praise (yup). I've been hassled this term, finishing a manuscript, and so haven't given their journals the attention I should have, and for that I'm called—quite civilly, though—to account. Overall, I get off pretty well.

Yet I have to admit that I do not much like the image of myself that emerges from these forms, the image of knowledgeable, humorous detachment and bland tolerance. I do not like the forms themselves, with their number ratings, reminiscent of the sheets circulated after the TV pilot has just played to its sample audience in Burbank. Most of all I dislike the attitude of calm consumer expertise that pervades the responses. I'm disturbed by the serene belief that my function—and, more important, Freud's, or Shakespeare's, or Blake's—is to divert, entertain, and interest. Observes one respondent, not at all unrepresentative: "Edmundson has done a fantastic job of presenting this difficult, important & controversial material in an enjoyable and approachable way."

Thanks but no thanks. I don't teach to amuse, to divert, or

even, for that matter, to be merely interesting. When someone says she "enjoyed" the course—and that word crops up again and again in my evaluations—somewhere at the edge of my immediate complacency I feel encroaching self-dislike. That is not at all what I had in mind. The off-the-wall questions and the sidebar jokes are meant as lead-ins to stronger stuff—in the case of the Freud course, to a complexly tragic view of life. But the affability and the one-liners often seem to be all that land with the students; their journals and evaluations leave me little doubt.

I want some of them to say that they've been changed by the course. I want them to measure themselves against what they've read. It's said that some time ago a Columbia University instructor used to issue a harsh two-part question. One: What book did you most dislike in the course? Two: What intellectual or characterological flaws in you does that dislike point to? The hand that framed those questions was surely heavy. But at least they compel one to see intellectual work as a confrontation between two people, student and author, where the stakes matter. Those Columbia students were being asked to relate the quality of an *encounter*, not rate the action as though it had unfolded on the big screen.

Why are my students describing the Oedipus complex and the death drive as being interesting and enjoyable to contemplate? And why am I coming across as an urbane, mildly ironic, endlessly affable guide to this intellectual territory, operating without intensity, generous, funny, and loose?

Because that's what works. On evaluation day, I reap the rewards of my partial compliance with the culture of my students and, too, with the culture of the university as it now operates. It's a culture that's gotten little exploration. Current critics tend to think that liberal arts education is in crisis because universities have been invaded by professors with peculiar ideas: deconstruction, Lacanianism, feminism, queer theory. They believe that genius and tradition are out and that PC, multiculturalism, and identity politics are in because of an invasion by tribes of tenured radicals, the late-millennial equivalents of the Visigoth hordes that cracked Rome's walls.

But mulling over my evaluations and then trying to take a hard, extended look at campus life both here at the University of Virginia and around the country eventually led me to some different conclusions. To me, liberal arts education is as ineffective as it is now not chiefly because there are a lot of strange theories in the air. (Used well, those theories *can* be illuminating.) Rather, it's that university culture, like American culture writ large, is, to put it crudely, ever more devoted to consumption and entertainment, to the using and using up of goods and images. For someone growing up in America now, there are few available alternatives to the cool consumer worldview. My students didn't ask for that view, much less create it, but they bring a consumer weltanschauung to school, where it exerts a powerful, and largely unacknowledged, influence. If we want to understand current universities, with their multiple woes, we might try leaving the realms of expert debate and fine ideas and turning to the classrooms and campuses, where a new kind of weather is gathering.

From time to time I bump into a colleague in the corridor and we have what I've come to think of as a Joon Lee fest. Joon Lee is one of the best students I've taught. He's endlessly curious, has read a small library's worth and seen every movie, and knows all about showbiz and entertainment. For a class of mine he wrote an essay using Nietzsche's Apollo and Dionysus to analyze the pop group the Supremes. A trite, cultural-studies bonbon? Not at all. He said striking things about conceptions of race in America and about how they shape our ideas of beauty. When I talk with one of his other teachers, we run on about the general splendors of his work and presence. But what inevitably follows a JL fest is a mournful reprise about the divide that separates him and a few other remarkable students from their contemporaries. It's not that some aren't nearly as bright—in terms of intellectual ability, my students are all that I could ask for. Instead, it's that Joon Lee has decided to follow his interests and let them make him into a singular and rather eccentric man; in his charming way, he doesn't mind being at odds with most anyone.

It's his capacity for enthusiasm that sets Joon apart from what I've come to think of as the reigning generational style. Whether the students are sorority/fraternity types, grunge aficionados, piercer/tattooers, black or white, rich or middle class (alas, I teach almost no students from truly poor backgrounds), they are, nearly across the board, very, very self-contained. On good days they display a light, appealing glow; on bad days, shuffling disgruntlement. But there's little fire, little passion to be found.

This point came home to me a few weeks ago when I was wandering across the university grounds. There, beneath a classically cast portico, were two students, male and female, having a rip-roaring argument. They were incensed, bellowing at each other, headstrong, confident, and wild. It struck me how rarely I see this kind of full-out feeling in students anymore. Strong emotional display is forbidden. When conflicts arise, it's generally understood that one of the parties will say something sarcastically propitiating ("Whatever" often does it) and slouch away.

How did my students reach this peculiar state in which all passion seems to be spent? I think that many of them have imbibed their sense of self from consumer culture in general and from the tube in particular. They're the progeny of a hundred cable channels and videos on demand. TV, Marshall McLuhan famously said, is a cool medium. Those who play best on it are low-key and nonassertive; they blend in. Enthusiasm, a la Joon Lee, quickly looks absurd. The form of character that's most appealing on TV is calmly self-interested though never greedy, attuned to the conventions, and ironic. Judicious timing is preferred to sudden self-assertion. The TV medium is inhospitable to inspiration, improvisation, failures, slipups. All must run perfectly.

Naturally, a cool youth culture is a marketing bonanza for producers of the right products, who do all they can to enlarge that culture and keep it grinding. The Internet, TV, and magazines now teem with what I call persona ads, ads for Nikes and Reeboks and Jeeps and Blazers that don't so much endorse the capacities of the product per se as show you what sort of person you will be once you've acquired it. The Jeep ad that features hip, outdoorsy kids whipping a Frisbee from mountaintop to mountaintop isn't so much about what Jeeps can do as it is about the kind of people who own them. Buy a Jeep and be one with them. The ad is of little consequence in itself, but expand its message exponentially and you have the central thrust of current consumer culture—buy in order to be.

Most of my students seem desperate to blend in, to look right, not to make a spectacle of themselves. (Do I have to tell you that those two students having the argument under the portico turned out to be acting in a role-playing game?) The specter of the uncool creates a subtle tyranny. It's apparently an easy standard to subscribe to, this Letterman-like, Tarantino-inflected cool, but once committed to it, you discover that matters are rather different. You're inhibited from showing emotion, stifled from trying to achieve anything original. You're made to feel that even the slightest departure from the reigning code will get you genially ostracized. This is a culture tensely committed to a laid-back norm.

Am I coming off like something of a crank here? Maybe. Oscar Wilde, who is almost never wrong, suggested that it is perilous to promiscuously contradict people who are much younger than yourself. Point taken. But one of the lessons that consumer hype tries to insinuate is that we must never rebel against the new, never even question it. If it's new—a new need, a new product, a new show, a new style, a new generation—it must be good. So maybe, even at the risk of winning the withered, brown laurels of crankdom, it pays to resist newness worship and cast a colder eye.

Praise for my students? I have some of that too. What my students are, at their best, is decent. They are potent believers in equality. They help out at the soup kitchen and volunteer to tutor poor kids to get a stripe on their résumés, sure. But they also want other people to have a fair shot. And in their commitment to fairness they are discerning; there you see them at their intellectual best. If I were on trial and innocent, I'd want them on the jury.

What they will not generally do, though, is indict the current system. They won't talk, say, about how the exigencies of capitalism lead to a reserve army of the unemployed and nearly inevitable misery. That would be getting too loud, too brash. For the pervading view is the cool consumer perspective, where passion and strong admiration are forbidden. "To stand in awe of nothing, Numicus, is perhaps the one and only thing that can make a man happy and keep him so," says Horace in the *Epistles*, and I fear that his lines ought to hang as a motto over the university gates in this era of high consumer capitalism.

It's easy to mount one's high horse and blame the students for this state of affairs. But they didn't create the present culture of consumption. (It was largely my own generation, that of the sixties, that let the counterculture's search for pleasure devolve into a quest for commodities.) And they weren't the ones responsible, when they were six and seven and eight years old, for unplugging the TV set from time to time or for hauling off and kicking a hole through it. It's my generation of parents who sheltered these students, kept them away from the hard knocks of everyday life, making them cautious and overfragile. It was their parents who demanded that teachers, from grade school on, flatter them endlessly so that kids are shocked if their college profs don't reflexively suck up to them.

Of course, the current generational style isn't simply derived from culture and environment. It's also about dollars. Students worry that taking too many chances with their education will sabotage their future prospects. They're aware of the fact that a drop that looks more and more like one wall of the Grand Canyon separates the top economic tenth from the rest of the population. There's a sentiment currently afoot that if you step aside for a moment to write, to travel, to fall too hard in love, you might lose position permanently. We may be on a conveyor belt, but it's worse down there on the filth-strewn factory floor. So don't sound off, don't blow your chance.

But wait. I teach at the famously conservative University of Virginia. Can I extend my view from Charlottesville to encompass the whole country, a whole generation of college students?

I can only say that I hear comparable stories about classroom life from colleagues everywhere in America. When I visit other schools to lecture, I see a similar scene unfolding. There are, of course, terrific students everywhere. And they're all the better for the way they've had to strive against the existing conformity. At some of the small liberal arts colleges, the tradition of strong engagement persists. But overall, the students strike me as being sweet and sad, hovering in a nearly suspended animation.

Too often now the pedagogical challenge is to make a lot from a little. Teaching Wordsworth's "Tintern Abbey," you ask for comments. No one responds. So you call on Stephen. Stephen: "The sound, this poem really flows." You: "Stephen seems interested in the music of the poem. We might extend his comment to ask if the poem's music coheres with its argument. Are they consistent? Or is there an emotional pain submerged here that's contrary to the poem's appealing melody?" All right, it's not usually that bad. But close. One friend describes it as rebound teaching: They proffer a weightless comment, you hit it back for all you're worth, then it comes wafting out again. Occasionally a professor will try to explain away this intellectual timidity by describing the students as perpetrators of postmodern irony, a highly sophisticated mode. Everything's a slick counterfeit, a simulacrum, so by no means should any phenomenon be taken seriously. But the students don't have the urbane, Oscar Wilde–type demeanor that goes with this view. Oscar was cheerful, funny, confident, strange. (Wilde, mortally ill, living in a Paris flophouse: "My wallpaper and I are fighting a duel to the death. One of the other of us has to go.") This generation's style is considerate, easy to please, and a touch depressed.

Granted, you might say, the kids come to school immersed in a consumer mentality—they're good Americans, after all—but then the university and the professors do everything in their power to fight that dreary mind-set in the interest of higher ideals, right? So it should be. But let us look at what is actually coming to pass.

Over the past few years, the physical layout of my university has been changing. Our funds go to construction, into new dorms, into renovating the student union. We have a new aquatics center and ever-improving gyms stocked with StairMasters and Nautilus machines. Engraved on the wall in the gleaming aquatics building is a line by our founder, Thomas Jefferson, declaring that everyone ought to get about two hours' exercise a day. Clearly even the author of the Declaration of Independence endorses the turning of his university into a sports-and-fitness emporium.

But such improvements shouldn't be surprising. Universities need to attract the best (that is, the smartest *and* the richest) students in order to survive in an ever more competitive market. Schools want kids whose parents can pay the full freight, not the ones who need scholarships or want to bargain down the tuition costs. If the marketing surveys say that the kids require sports centers, then, trustees willing, they shall have them. In fact, as I began looking around, I came to see that more and more of what's going on in the university is customer driven. The consumer pressures that beset me on evaluation day are only a part of an overall trend.

From the start, the contemporary university's relationship with students has a solicitous, nearly servile tone. As soon as someone enters his junior year in high school, and especially if he's living in a prosperous zip code, the informational material—the advertising—comes flooding in. Pictures, testimonials, videocassettes, and CD-ROMs (some bidden, some not) arrive at the door from colleges across the country, all trying to capture the student and his tuition cash. The freshman-to-be sees photos of well-appointed dorm rooms; of elaborate phys-ed facilities; of fine dining rooms; of expertly kept sports fields; of orchestras and drama troupes; of students working alone (no overbearing grown-ups in range), peering with high seriousness into computers and microscopes; or of students arrayed outdoors in attractive conversational garlands.

Occasionally—but only occasionally, for we usually photograph rather badly; in appearance we tend at best to be styleless—there's a professor teaching a class. (The college catalogues I received, by my request only, in the late sixties were austere affairs full of professors' credentials and course descriptions; it was clear on whose terms the enterprise was going to unfold.) As that perhaps too candid college financial officer told me: Colleges don't have admissions offices anymore, they have marketing departments. Is it surprising that someone who has been approached with photos and tapes, bells and whistles, might come in thinking that the Freud and Shakespeare she had signed up to study were also going to be agreeable treats?

How did we reach this point? In part the answer is a matter of demographics and (surprise) of money. Aided by the GI bill, the college-going population in America dramatically increased after the Second World War. Then came the baby boomers, and to accommodate them, schools continued to grow. Universities expand easily enough, but with tenure locking faculty in for lifetime jobs, and with the general reluctance of administrators to eliminate their own slots, it's not easy for a university to contract. So after the baby boomers had passed through, the colleges turned to energetic promotional strategies to fill the empty chairs. And suddenly (college became a buyer's market.) What students and their parents wanted had to be taken more and more into account. That usually meant creating more comfortable, less challenging environments, places where almost no one failed, everything was enjoyable, and everyone was nice.

Just as universities must compete with one another for students, so must the individual departments. At a time of rank economic anxiety, the English and history majors have to contend for students against the purportedly more success-insuring branches, such as the sciences and commerce. In 1968, more than 21 percent of all the bachelor's degrees conferred in America were in the humanities; by 1993, that number had fallen to about 13 percent. The humanities now must struggle to attract students, many of whose parents devoutly wish they would study something else.

One of the ways we've tried to stay attractive is by loosening up. We grade more indulgently than our colleagues in science. In English, we don't give many D's, or C's for that matter. (It's possible that the rigors of Chem 101 create almost as many English majors per year as the splendors of Shakespeare.) A professor at Stanford explained grade inflation in the humanities by observing that the undergraduates were getting smarter every year; the higher grades simply recorded how much better they were than their predecessors. Sure.

Along with softening the grades, many humanities departments have relaxed major requirements. There are some good reasons for introducing more choice into curricula and requiring fewer standard courses. But the move, like many others in the university now, jibes with a tendency to serve—and not challenge—the students. Students can also float in and out of classes during the first two weeks of each term without making any commitment. The common name of this time span—shopping period—speaks volumes about the consumer mentality that's in play. Usually, too, the kids can drop courses up until the last month with only an innocuous "W," for "withdraw," on their transcripts. Does a course look too challenging? No problem. Take it pass-fail. A happy consumer is, by definition, one with multiple options, one who can always have what he wants. And since a course is something the students and their parents have bought and paid cash for, why can't they do with it pretty much as they please?

A sure result of the university's widening elective leeway is to give students more power over their teachers. Those who don't like you can simply avoid you. If the clientele dislikes you en masse, you can be left without students, period. My first term teaching I walked into my introduction to poetry course and found it inhabited by two students, one of whom was the gloriously named Bambi Lynn Dean. Bambi and I chatted amiably awhile, but for all that she and the pleasure of her name could offer, I was on the way to meltdown. It was all a mistake, luckily, a problem with the scheduling book. Everyone was waiting for me next door. But in a dozen years of teaching I haven't forgotten that feeling of being ignominiously marooned. For it happens to others, and not always because of scheduling glitches. I've seen older colleagues go through hot embarrassment at not having enough students sign up for their courses: They graded too hard, demanded too much, had beliefs too far out of keeping with the existing disposition. It takes only a few such instances to draw other members of the professoriat into line.

And if what's called tenure reform—which generally just means the abolition of tenure—is broadly enacted, professors will be yet more vulnerable to the whims of their customer-students. Teach what pulls the kids in, or walk. What about entire departments that don't deliver? If the kids say no to Latin and Greek, is it time to dissolve classics? Such questions are being entertained more and more seriously by university administrators.

How does one prosper with the present clientele? Many of the most successful professors are the ones who have "decentered" their classrooms. There's an emphasis on group projects and on computer-generated exchanges among the students. What they seem to want most is to talk to one another. A classroom now is frequently an "environment," a place highly conducive to the exchange of existing ideas, the students' ideas. Listening to one another, students sometimes change their opinions. But what they generally can't do is acquire a new vocabulary, a new perspective, that will cast issues in a fresh light.

The Socratic method—the animated, sometimes impolite give-and-take between student and teacher—seems too jagged for current sensibilities. Students frequently come to my office to tell me how intimidated they feel in class; the thought of being embarrassed in front of the group fills them with dread. I remember a student telling me how humiliating it was to be corrected by the teacher, by me. So I asked the logical question: "Should I let a major factual error go by to save discomfort?" The student—a good student, smart and earnest—said that was a tough question. He'd need to think about it.

Disturbing? Sure. But I wonder, are we really getting students ready for Socratic exchange with professors when we push them off into vast lecture rooms, two and three hundred to a class, sometimes face them with only grad students until their third year, and signal in our myriad professorial ways that we often have much better things to do than sit in our offices and talk with them? How bad will the student-faculty ratios have to become, how teeming the lecture courses, before we hear students righteously complaining, as they did thirty years ago, about the impersonality of their schools, about their decline into knowledge factories? "This is a firm," said Mario Savio at Berkeley during the Free Speech protests of the sixties, "and if the Board of Regents are the board of directors . . . then . . . the faculty are a bunch of employees and we're the raw material. But we're a bunch of raw material that don't mean . . . to be made into any product."

Teachers who really do confront students, who provide significant challenges to what they believe, *can* be very successful, granted. But sometimes such professors generate more than a little trouble for themselves. A controversial teacher can send students hurrying to the deans and the counselors, claiming to have been offended. (*Offensive* is the preferred term of repugnance today, just as *enjoyable* is the summit of praise.) Colleges have brought in hordes of counselors and deans to make sure that everything is smooth, serene, unflustered, that everyone has a good time. To the counselor, to the dean, and to the university legal squad, that which is normal, healthy, and prudent is best.

An air of caution and deference is everywhere. When my students come to talk with me in my office, they often exhibit a Franciscan humility. "Do you have a moment?" "I know you're busy. I won't take up much of your time." Their presences tend to be very light; they almost never change the temperature of the room. The dress is nondescript: Clothes are in earth tones; shoes are practical—cross-trainers, hiking boots, work shoes, Dr. Martens, with now and then a stylish pair of raised-sole boots on one of the young women. Many, male and female both, peep from beneath the bills of monogramed baseball caps. Quite a few wear sports, or even corporate, logos, sometimes on one piece of clothing but occasionally (and disconcertingly) on more. The walk is slow; speech is careful, sweet, a bit weary, and without strong inflection. (After the first lively week of the term, most seem far in debt to sleep.) They are almost unfailingly polite. They don't want to offend me; I could hurt them, savage their grades.

Naturally, there are exceptions, kids I chat animatedly with, who offer a joke, or go on about this or that new CD (almost never a book, no). But most of the traffic is genially sleepwalking. I have to admit that I'm a touch wary, too. I tend to hold back. An unguarded remark, a joke that's taken to be off-color, or simply an uncomprehended comment can lead to difficulties. I keep it literal. They disturb me a little, these kind and melancholy students, who themselves seem rather frightened of their own lives.

Before they arrive, we ply the students with luscious ads, guaranteeing them a cross between summer camp and lotusland. When they get here, flattery and nonstop entertainment are available, if that's what they want. And when they leave? How do we send our students out into the world? More and more, our administrators call the booking agents and line up one or another celebrity to usher the graduates into the future. Recently Kermit the Frog won himself an honorary degree at Southampton College on Long Island; Bruce Willis and Yogi Berra took credentials away at Montclair State; Arnold Schwarzenegger scored at the University of Wisconsin–Superior. At Wellesley, Oprah Winfrey gave the commencement address.

(*Wellesley*—one of the most rigorous academic colleges in the nation.) At the University of Vermont, Whoopi Goldberg laid down the word. But why should a worthy administrator contact someone who might actually say something, something disturbing, something "offensive," when he can get what the parents and kids apparently want and what the newspapers will softly commend—more lite entertainment, more TV?

Is it a surprise, then, that this generation of students—steeped in consumer culture before going off to school, treated as potent customers well before their date of arrival, then pandered to from day one until the morning of the final kiss-off from Kermit or one of his kin—are inclined to see the books they read as a string of entertainments to be placidly enjoyed or languidly cast down? Given the way universities are now administered (which is more and more to say, given the way that they are currently marketed), is it a shock that the kids don't come to school hot to learn, unable to bear their own ignorance? For some measure of self-dislike, or self-discontent—which is much different from simple depression—is a prerequisite for getting an education that matters. My students, alas, usually lack the confidence to acknowledge what would be their most precious asset for learning: their ignorance.

One day I asked my Freud class a question that never fails to solicit intriguing responses: Who are your heroes? Whom do you admire? After one remarkable answer, featuring T.S. Eliot as hero, a series of generic replies rolled in, one gray wave after the next: my father, my best friend, a doctor who lives in our town, my high school history teacher. Virtually all the heroes were people my students had known personally, people who had done something local, specific, and practical—and had done it *for them*. They were good people, unselfish people, these heroes, but most of all they were people who had delivered the goods.

My students' answers didn't exhibit any philosophical resistance to the idea of greatness. It's not that they had been primed by their professors with complex arguments to combat the notion of genius or any other form of human distinction. For the truth is that these students don't need debunking theories. Long before college, skepticism became their habitual mode. They are the progeny of the hypercool ethos of the box. It's inane to say that theorizing professors have created them, as many conservative critics like to do. Rather, they have substantially created a university environment in which facile skepticism can thrive without being substantially contested.

Skeptical approaches have *potential* value. If you have no all-encompassing religious faith, no faith in historical destiny or the future of the West or anything comparably grand, you need to acquire your vision of the world somewhere. If it's from literature, then the various visions literature offers have to be inquired into skeptically. Surely it matters that women are denigrated in Milton and in Pope; that some novelistic voices assume an overbearing godlike authority; that the poor are, in this or that writer, inevitably cast as clowns. You can't buy all of literature wholesale if it's going to help draw your patterns of belief.

But demystifying theories are now overused, applied mechanically. It's all logocentrism, patriarchy, ideology. And in this the student environment—laid-back, skeptical, knowing—is, I believe, central. Full-out debunking is what plays with this clientele. Some have been doing it nearly as long as, if more crudely than, their deconstructionist teachers. In the context of the contemporary university and cool consumer culture, a useful intellectual skepticism has become exaggerated into a fundamentalist caricature of itself. The teachers have buckled to their students' views.

At its best, multiculturalism can be attractive as well-deployed theory. What could be more valuable than encountering the best work of far-flung cultures and becoming a citizen of the world? But in the current consumer environment, where flattery plays so well, the urge to encounter the other can devolve into the urge to find others who embody and celebrate the right ethnic origins. So we put aside the African novelist Chinua Achebe's abrasive, troubling *Things Fall Apart* and gravitate toward hymns on Africa, cradle of all civilizations.

What about the phenomenon called political correctness? Raising the standard of civility and tolerance in the university has been—who can deny it?—a very good thing. Yet this admirable impulse has expanded to the point where one is enjoined to speak well—and only well—of women, blacks, gays, the disabled, in fact of virtually everyone. And we can owe this expansion in many ways to the student culture. Students now do not wish to be criticized, not in any form. (The culture of consumption never criticizes them, at least not *overtly*.) In the current university, the movement for urbane tolerance has devolved into an imperative against critical reaction, turning much of the intellectual life into a dreary Sargasso Sea. At a certain point, professors stopped being usefully sensitive and became more like careful retailers who have it as a cardinal point of doctrine never to piss the customer off.

To some professors, the solution lies in the movement called cultural studies. What students need, they believe, is to form a critical perspective on pop culture. It's a fine idea, no doubt.

Students should be able to run a critical commentary against the stream of consumer stimulations in which they're immersed. But cultural studies programs rarely work, because no matter what you propose by way of analysis, things tend to bolt downhill toward an uncritical discussion of students' tastes, into what they like and don't like. If you want to do a Frankfurt School–style analysis of *Braveheart*, you can be pretty sure that by midclass Adorno and Horkheimer will be consigned to the junk heap of history and you'll be collectively weighing the charms of Mel Gibson. One sometimes wonders if cultural studies hasn't prospered because, under the guise of serious intellectual analysis, it gives the customers what they most want—easy pleasure, more TV. Cultural studies becomes nothing better than what its detractors claim it is—Madonna studies—when students kick loose from the critical perspective and groove to the product, and that, in my experience teaching film and pop culture, happens plenty.

On the issue of genius, as on multiculturalism and political correctness, we professors of the humanities have, I think, also failed to press back against our students' consumer tastes. Here we tend to nurse a pair of—to put it charitably—disparate views. In one mode, we're inclined to a programmatic debunking criticism. We call the concept of genius into question. But in our professional lives per se, we aren't usually disposed against the idea of distinguished achievement. We argue animatedly about the caliber of potential colleagues. We support a star system in which some professors are far better paid and teach less under better conditions than the rest. In our own profession, we are creating a system that is the mirror image of the one we're dismantling in the curriculum. Ask a professor what she thinks of the work of Stephen Greenblatt, a leading critic of

Shakespeare, and you'll hear it for an hour. Ask her what her views are on Shakespeare's genius and she's likely to begin questioning the term along with the whole "discourse of evaluation." This dual sensibility may be intellectually incoherent. But in its awareness of what plays with students, it's conducive to good classroom evaluations and, in its awareness of where and how the professional bread is buttered, to self-advancement as well.

My overall point is this: It's not that a left-wing professorial coup has taken over the university. It's that at American universities, left-liberal politics have collided with the ethos of consumerism. The consumer ethos is winning.

Then how do those who at least occasionally promote genius and high literary ideals look to current students? How do we appear, those of us who imagine that if you give yourself over completely to your subject you'll be rewarded with insight beyond what you individually command?

I'm reminded of an old piece of newsreel footage I saw once. The speaker (perhaps it was Lenin, maybe Trotsky) was haranguing a large crowd. He was expostulating, arm-waving, carrying on. Whether it was flawed technology or the man himself, I'm not sure, but the orator looked like an intricate mechanical device that had sprung into fast-forward. To my students, who mistrust enthusiasm in every form, that's me when I start riffing about Freud or Blake. But more and more, as my evaluations showed, I've been replacing evaluation and intellectual animation with stand-up routines, keeping it all at arm's length, praising under the cover of irony.

It's too bad that the idea of genius has been denigrated so far, because it actually offers a live alternative to the demoralizing culture of hip in which most of my students are mired. By embracing the works and lives of extraordinary people, you can adapt new ideals to revise those that came courtesy of your parents, your neighborhood, your clan—or the tube. The aim of a good liberal arts education was once, to adapt an observation by the scholar Walter Jackson Bate, to see that "we need not be the passive victims of what we deterministically call 'circumstances' (social, cultural, or reductively psychological-personal), but that by linking ourselves through what Keats calls an 'immortal free-masonry' with the great we can become freer— freer to be ourselves, to be what we most want and value."

But genius isn't just a personal standard; genius can also have political effect. To me, one of the best things about democratic thinking is the conviction that genius can spring up anywhere. Walt Whitman is born into the working class and thirty-six years later we have a poetic image of America that gives a passionate dimension to the legalistic brilliance of the Constitution. A democracy needs to constantly develop, and to do so it requires the most powerful visionary minds to interpret the present and to propose possible shapes for the future. By continuing to notice and praise genius, we create a culture in which the kind of poetic gamble that Whitman made—a gamble in which failure would have entailed rank humiliation, depression, maybe suicide—still takes place. By rebelling against established ways of seeing and saying things, genius helps us to apprehend how malleable the present is and how promising the future. If we teachers do not endorse genius and self-overcoming, can we be surprised when our students find their ideal images in TV's latest persona ads?

A world uninterested in genius is a despondent place, whose sad denizens drift from coffee bar to Prozac dispensary, unfired by ideals or the glowing image of the self that one might become. As Northrop Frye says in a beautiful and now dramatically unfashionable sentence, "The artist who uses the same energy and genius that Homer and Isaiah had will find that he not only lives in the same palace of art as Homer and Isaiah, but lives in it at the same time." We ought not to deny the existence of such a place simply because we, or those we care for, find the demands it makes intimidating, the rent too high.

What happens if we keep trudging along this bleak course? What happens if our most intelligent students never learn to strive to overcome what they are? What if genius, and the imitation of genius, become silly, outmoded ideas? What you're likely to get are more and more two-dimensional men and women. These will be people who live for easy pleasures, for comfort and prosperity, who think of money first, then second, and third, who hug the status quo; people who believe in God as a sort of insurance policy (cover your bets); people who are never surprised. They will be people so pleased with themselves (when they're not in despair at the general pointlessness of their lives) that they cannot imagine humanity could do better. They'll think it their highest duty to clone themselves as frequently as possible. They'll claim to be happy, and they'll live a long time.

It is probably time now to offer a spate of inspiring solutions. Here ought to come a list of reforms, with due notations about a core curriculum and various requirements. What the traditionalists who offer such solutions miss is that no matter what our current students are given to read, many of them will simply translate it into melodrama, with flat characters and predictable morals. (The unabated capitalist culture that conservative critics so often endorse has put students in a position to do little else.)

One can't simply wave a curricular wand and reverse accul-turation.

Perhaps it would be a good idea to try firing the counselors and sending half the deans back into their classrooms, disman-tling the football team and making the stadium into a playground for local kids, emptying the fraternities and boarding up the student-activities office. Such measures would convey the mes-sage that American colleges are not northern outposts of Club Med. A willingness on the part of the faculty to defy student con-viction and affront them occasionally—to be usefully offensive—also might not be a bad thing. We professors talk a lot about subversion, which generally means subverting the views of people who never hear us talk or read our work. But to subvert the views of our students—our customers—that would be something else again.

Ultimately, though, it is up to individuals—and individual students in particular—to make their own way against the cur-rent sludgy tide. There's still the library, still the museum, there's still the occasional teacher who lives to find things greater than herself to admire. There are still fellow students who have not been cowed. Universities are inefficient, cluttered, archaic places, with many unguarded corners where one can open a book or gaze out onto the larger world and construe it freely. Those who do as much, trusting themselves against the weight of cur-rent opinion, will have contributed something to bringing this sad dispensation to an end. As for myself, I'm canning my low-key one-liners; when the kids' TV-based tastes come to the fore, I'll aim and shoot. And when it's time to praise genius, I'll try to do it in the right style, full-out, with faith that finer artistic spirits (maybe not Homer and Isaiah quite, but close, close), still alive somewhere in the ether, will help me out when my invention flags, the students doze, or the dean mutters into the phone. I'm getting back to a more exuberant style; I'll be expostulating and arm-waving straight into the millennium, yes I will.

DWELLING IN POSSIBILITIES (2008)

A T THE BEGINNING of school last fall, I ran into a student out on the University of Virginia Lawn, not far from the famous statue of Homer instructing an admiring pupil. Homer's student is in a toga. Mine was wearing wrap-around sunglasses like Bono's, black jeans, and a red T-shirt emblazoned with white Chinese characters. Over his shoulder he carried his laptop.

We asked each other the usual question: What did you do over the summer? What he did, as I recall, was a brief internship at a well-regarded Internet publication, a six-country swing though Europe, then back to enjoy his family and home, reconnect with high school friends, and work on recording a rock CD. What had I done? I had written five drafts of a chapter for a book on the last two years of Sigmund Freud's life. I had traveled to Crozet, a few miles away, to get pizza. I'd traveled 150 miles to Virginia Beach the day after I woke up distressed because I couldn't figure out how to begin my chapter. I stayed a night at the beach, figured it out (I thought), and come home. My young friend looked at me with a mixture of awe and compassion. I felt a little like one of those aged men of the earth who populate Wordsworth's poetry. One of them, the Old Cumberland Beggar, goes so slowly that you never actually see him move, but if you return to the spot where you first encountered him two hours ago, lo, he has gone a little way down the road. The footprints are there to prove it.

I headed back to my office for draft number six, or something comparably glamorous. Where was my student going? He was no doubt heading into a more turbo-charged version of his summer, a life of supreme intensity created in collaboration with the laptop slung over his shoulder. For his student generation is a singular one: Its members have a spectacular hunger for life and more life. They want to study (a little), travel, make friends, make more friends, take in all the movies, listen to every hot band, keep up with everyone they've ever known. And there's something else, too, that distinguishes them: They live to multiply possibilities. They're enemies of closure. For as much as they want to do and actually manage to do, they always strive to keep their options open, never to shut possibilities down.

This hunger for life has a number of consequences, for now and for the future. It's part of what makes this student generation appealing, highly promising—and also vulnerable and dangerous. These students may go on to do great and good things, but they also present risks to themselves and to the common future. They seem almost to have been created, as the poet says, "half to rise and half to fall." As a teacher of theirs (and fellow citizen), I'm more than a little concerned about which it's going to be.

Internet technology was on hand for my current students from about 1995, when the Netscape browser made the Internet accessible to everyone. And the Internet seems to me to have shaped their generation as much as the multichannel TV—with that critical device, the remote control—shaped the students who registered for my classes a decade earlier. What is the Internet to current students?

Consider first what it is not. A friend of mine who has assiduously kept a journal for forty years calls the journal, which now runs to about forty volumes, a "life thickener." His quotations, pictures, clips, drawings, and paintings give dense meaning to the blind onrush that unexamined life can be. He looks back through the volumes and sees that there *was* a life and that to him it meant something. To my students, I suspect, my friend would look like a medieval monk laboring over his manuscripts, someone with a radically pre-postmodern feel for time, someone who did not, in fact, understand what time actually is.

An Internet-linked laptop, one may safely say, is not a life thickener. At the fingertips of my students the laptop is a multiplier of the possible. "I dwell in possibility," says Emily Dickinson, "a fairer house than prose." My students want to dwell there with her. Just as TV and the culture of cool slowed kids down, made them languid and a bit shell-shocked, the Internet has had the effect of speeding them up.

My university recently passed an edict: No one, dammit (insofar as edicts can say dammit), is going to triple-major. Everyone now who is worth his tuition money double majors: The students in my classes are engineering/English, politics/English, chemistry/English. An urban legend in my leaf-fringed 'hood is that someone got around this inane dictum about triple majors by majoring in four subjects—there was, it seems, no rule against that. The top students in my school, the ones who set the standard for the rest even if they drive the rest crazy, want to take eight classes a term, major promiscuously, have a semester abroad at three different schools, connect with every likely person who is on Facebook, be checked in with by their pals and check in at every living moment.

One day I tried an experiment in a class I was teaching on English and American Romanticism. We had been studying Thoreau and talking about his reflections (sour) on the uses of technology for communication. ("We are in great haste," he says, "to construct a magnetic telegraph from Maine to Texas; but Maine and Texas, it may be, have nothing important to communicate.") I asked the group, "How many places were you simultaneously yesterday—at the most?" Suppose you were chatting on your cell phone, partially watching a movie in one corner of a computer screen, texting with three people (a modest number), and glancing occasionally at the text for some other course than ours—grazing, maybe, in Samuelson's *Economics* rather than diving deep into Thoreau's "Economy"—and then, also, tossing the occasional word to your roommate? That would be seven, seven places at once. Some students—with a little high-spirited hyperbole thrown in, no doubt—got into double digits. Of course it wouldn't take the Dalai Lama or Henry David Thoreau to assure them that anyone who is in seven places at once is not anywhere in particular—not present, not here now. Be everywhere now—that's what the current technology invites, and that's what my students apparently aspire to do.

Internet-linked computers are desiring-machines—machines for the stimulation of desire. But so is a TV; so in a certain sense is a movie screen. What makes the Internet singular is its power to expand desire, expand possibility beyond the confines of prior media. (My students are possibility junkies.) You can multiply the number of possible clothing purchases near to infinity and do it with stunning speed. You can make all the pleated skirts in the world appear almost all at once for you to choose from. As we talked about this in class—with Thoreau's disapproving specter looking on (sometimes it appears that Thoreau disapproves of everything, except the drinking of cold water)—something surprising came out. The moment of maximum Internet pleasure was not the moment of closure, when you sealed the deal; it was the moment when the choices had been multiplied to the highest sum. It was the moment of maximum promise, when you touched the lip of the possible: of four majors and eight courses per term and a gazillion hits on your Facebook page, and being everyplace (almost) at once, and gazing upon all the pleated skirts that the world doth hold.

This is what Immanuel Kant, were he around to see it, might have called the computer sublime. (He called something like it mathematical sublimity.) The moment when you make the purchase, close the deal, pick a girlfriend, set a date: All those things, the students around the Thoreau table concurred, were a letdown, consummations not really to be wished for. The students were a little surprised by the conclusions they came to about themselves. "It's when I can see it all in front of me," one young woman said, "that's when I'm the happiest."

Ask an American college student what he's doing on Friday night. Ask him at five thirty Friday afternoon. "I don't know" will likely be the first response. But then will come a list of possibilities to make the average Chinese menu look sullenly costive: the concert, the play, the movie, the party, the stay-at-home, the chilling ("chillaxing"), the monitoring of SportsCenter, the reading (fast, fast) of an assignment or two. University students now are virtual Hamlets of the virtual world, pondering possibility, faces pressed up against the sweetshop window of their all-purpose desiring machines. To ticket or not to ticket, buy or not to, party or no, or perhaps to simply stay in and to multiply options in numberless numbers, never to be closed down: Those are the questions.

And once you do get somewhere, wherever it might be, you'll find that, as Gertrude Stein has it, there's "no there there." At a student party, I'm told, about a fourth of the kids have their cell phones locked to their ears. What are they doing? "They're talking to their friends." About? "About another party they might conceivably go to." And naturally the other party is better than the one that they're now at (and not at), though of course there will be people at that party on their cell phones, talking about other simulacrum gatherings, spiraling on into M.C. Escher infinity.

It's possible that recent events in the world have added intensity to a student's quest for more possibilities. The events of September 11, which current college students experienced when they were eight, nine, ten, were an undoubted horror. But they had the effect, I think, of waking America's young people up from a pseudo-nihilistic doze. Before New York, Pennsylvania, and Virginia, the middle-class American teenager's world had been a pleasure dome full of rare delights. It was the reign of television: the oracle that knows everything and can take you anywhere. Television brought images of bliss, and its ads showed you the products that you needed to buy in order to achieve it. That well-known Jeep ad I mentioned in the last chapter that depicted hip kids tossing Frisbees and laughing like rock stars had nothing to do with the properties of a Jeep. It was a persona ad that advertised the sort of person you'd be when you acquired the product. The ad was an emblem of the consumer moment: Buy in order to be.

Students wanted to be cool. They wanted to be beyond reproach. There was a sense abroad that if you simply did what you were supposed to do, kept low to the ground and stayed on the conveyor belt, the future that TV promised would be yours. Everything was a mode of entertainment, or could be transformed into one after it had been submitted to Letterman-style ridicule. President Clinton was a genial boy from Arkansas who awoke one day and found himself in office. But that had not slaked his boyishness at all. He still wanted a version of what every boy did: all-nighters, pizza, and his pals in constant attendance. The president was a dog who couldn't stay on the porch. My students—the guys in particular—often found him the perfect image of success: You need never grow up; need never abandon college-boy mode. The couch where you sat, hours a day, monitoring TV in lordly condescension, would in time morph into an airship to swoosh you into your dreams.

But then there came the day of near–American Apocalypse, September 11, 2001. The prospect of hanging, Doctor Johnson observed, does wonders to concentrate the mind. The mind of America has been concentrated. No one believes that the whole edifice is likely to topple down around us soon. But everyone now lives charged with the knowledge that today, tomorrow, next week, we can suffer an event that will change everything drastically. A dirty bomb in the middle of a great city, poison wafting in sweet-smelling clouds through a subway system, a water supply subtly tainted: Such things would not only destroy the lives of those they touch directly, they'd discompose and remake America in ways that would be, to say the least, none too sweet. Tomorrow the deck may be shuffled and recut by the devil's hand. So what shall we do now?

The answer that comes from current students would seem to be this: Live, live, before the bombs go off in San Francisco or the water goes vile in New York and the new Mahdi appears on a billion screens at once to pronounce another turn in the Holy War that, for him, has been ongoing since the first Crusader scraped an armored foot on the soil of the Holy Land. On that bad day there will be, at the very least, the start of a comprehensive *closing down*. There will be no more free travel, no more easy money, and much less loose talk. Life will become a confinement, a prison, a pound. So now, as James's Strether instructs Little Bilham, you must "live all you can; it's a mistake not to." There's a humane hunger to my students' hustle for more life—but I think it's possible that down below bubbles a fear. Do it now, for later may be too late.

It's clearly a new university world that I'm living in, though it took me some time to see it. My revelation occurred a few months ago. Up until that point, I was always happy to see students bringing their laptops into class. The sight of them conjured up visions of upbeat news magazine covers: kids in ordered rows behind their computers, tapping in the new millennium. And the students who brought their laptops seemed to be the most engaged: They'd be skittering fast across the keys, alert and alive and glancing up from time to time to toss a few sentences into the conversation. These were the plugged-in kids, the committed ones. But then one day I made a rare trip to the blackboard and on the way glanced over a laptopper's shoulder. There was what appeared to be a YouTube video in one corner (Shakira? The "Hips Don't Lie" video?) and e-mail front and center, but nothing much to do with the subject of the class. How could I have missed it? This sort of thing is now the way of the classroom world.

Three thousand first-year students entered my university last year: Two thousand nine hundred and six of them—we keep some tight records here—brought laptops with them; ninety brought desktops. Four students—the incoming James Deans no doubt—showed up computerless. (Ten years ago, half of our first-year students came to school without computers.) At Virginia, as at just about every other university, almost all buildings are now equipped with wireless routers. This began to happen about four years ago, and many of us professors barely noticed it in part because we generally travel only from office to classroom. But our students are nomads, on the move all day. Wherever they sit, they set up Internet Command Central. Now students in almost any classroom can get directly onto the Internet and, given the shieldlike screens on their laptops, they can call up what they like. Especially in the big lecture classes, everyone's flitting from website to website, checking e-mail, and instant messaging. Do they pay any attention to the class? My students tell me that they're experts in paying attention to many things at once: It's no problem at all.

A romantic, says Nietzsche, is someone who always wants to be elsewhere: If that's so, then the children of the Internet are romantics, for they perpetually wish to be someplace else and the laptop reliably helps take them there. The e-mailer, the instant messenger, the Web browser are all dispersing their energies and interests outward, away from the present, the here and now. The Internet user is constantly connecting with people and institutions far away, creating surrogate communities that displace the potential community at hand.

Then, too, booking by computer has made travel easier and, by eliminating a certain number of middlemen, kept it reasonably cheap. So there's an inducement to take off physically as well. The Internet is perhaps the most centrifugal technology ever devised. The classroom, where you sit down in one space at one time and ponder a text or an issue in slow motion, is coming to feel ever more antiquated. What's at a premium now is movement, making connections, getting all the circuitry fizzing and popping.

For students now, life is elsewhere. Life is at parties, at clubs, in music, with friends, in sports, and on and on through the Internet. Classes matter to them (a little), but classes are just part of an ever-enlarging web of activities and diversions. Students now seek to master their work—not to be taken over by it and consumed. They want to dispatch it, do it quickly, cop a high grade, and then get on to the many things that truly interest them. For my students live in the future and not the present; they live with their prospects for success and pleasure. They dwell in possibility.

Drugs? Drugs are a big part of the game, along with the Internet. The answer to the question "What drugs are college students taking now?" is, as it has been for some time, "All of the above." But the drugs that have most recently entered the scene are the ones designed to combat attention deficit disorder: Adderall, Ritalin, Concerta, and Daytrana, which delivers the meds through a patch. These are all pharmaceuticals, obtained by prescription, though often the people taking them have never gotten diagnosed. The ADD drugs seem to be omnipresent; they're on sale in every dorm at prices that rise exponentially as the week of final exams approaches. "Twenty dollars for a hit," one student told me, "on the night before an exam in the intro econ class." Their effect is, pretty subtly but pretty surely, to speed the taker up. They kick him forward, give him fresh juice to keep exploring possibilities, to keep buying and doing and buying and doing.

The idea is to keep moving, never to stop. It's now become so commonplace as to be beneath notice, but there was a time that every city block contiguous to a university did not contain a shop dispensing a speed-you-up drug and inviting people to sit down and enjoy it along with wireless computer access. Laptops seem to go with coffee (and other stimulants) in much the same way that blood-and-gold sunsets went with LSD and Oreo cookies with weed. (It's possible, I sometimes think, that fully half of the urban Starbucks in America are located in rental properties that once were head shops.) Nor were there always energy drinks, vile-tasting concoctions coming in cans covered with superhero insignias designed to make you run as fast and steady as your computer, your car, and—this is Darwinian capitalism after all—your colleagues. You've got to keep going. Almost all of my students have one book—an old book—that they've read and treasured and read again. It's the American epic of free movement, *On the Road*, a half century old this year, but to them one of the few things in the culture of my generation that's still youthful.

The sports that this generation has put its stamp on, X Games sorts of things like snowboarding, surfing, and skateboarding, are all about velocity, motion, skimming. They're about speeding flawlessly through space without being diverted, slowed down, or captured by mere gravity. (Gravity, in all senses, is what my students are out to avoid.) Like the drugs, the sports help to keep the kids moving elsewhere.

How about their music? It's a little hard to say. Students no longer turn their speakers out the dorm window and blast the quad with Poco's *Deliverin'*. Music now comes personally, a whisper in the ear, through the iPod, so that everyone can walk around with the soundtrack to his own movie purring. This constant music plug-in is another mode of being elsewhere, about right for the current dispensation. As to the sort of music it is, the kind of stuff that runs through the iPods is varied. Many of my students delight in listening to bands that absolutely no one but they seem to have heard of. When I ask them in class to tell me their favorite tunes, I'm reminded of the days when my friends and I would show each other our baseball cards. As you flipped over yours, the other guy responded with "Got it. Got it. Don't got it. Got it." "Don't got it" came with a wince. The coolest kid in the room now is clearly the one whose favorite bands are the ones the others wince most over— the ones they don't got.

But the students have a collective musical taste, too. When they're together at a party, when they've unplugged their iPods and put their cell phones temporarily on vibrate, what they want is rap. Whatever the content of rap, its form is propulsive forward motion—the beat, the energy pulse, is what it's about. It drives you forward, runs fuel through the motor. Rap is part of the constant stimulation that students seem unable to live without.

When a seminar is over now, the students reach their hands into their pockets and draw—it looks like *Gunfight at the O.K. Corral*. But what they're reaching for—after discussing Thoreau, say, on the pleasures of solitude—are their cell phones. They've been disconnected, off the drug, for more than an hour and they need a fix. The cell phoning comes as a relief: The students have been (give or take) in one place, at one time, pondering a few passages from *Walden*. Now they need to disperse themselves again, get away from the immediate, dissolve the present away.

But I teach at one university, the University of Virginia, known for high-powered students who are also sometimes high partiers: Is what I'm saying true for all schools? Well, I do some traveling and talking to colleagues at other places, and from what I can tell, the more high-prestige the institution, the more frenetic and centrifugal the pace. At Harvard and Yale, I'd now expect to find kids who've hit a white incandescence or maybe who've fused completely with the Internet, living within it, like characters out of *Neuromancer*, finding in their merger with the machine a kind of high that can take the place of happiness.

Skate fast over the surfaces of life and cover all the extended space you can, says the new ethos. Perhaps the greatest of all surface skimmers, the poet laureate of the way we live now at college, was William Wordsworth's arch-antagonist, George Gordon, Lord Byron. The poetry of Wordsworth, the explorer of inner space, is deliberate, slow, ponderous, like those old men of the woods he loves to depict—and that I may resemble to my fast-skimming students. The complaint against Wordsworth is that he is tiresome; he has no time for sex or violence, just muted natural beauty and a mystical sublime. Byron—rich, beautiful, glamorous, with startlingly white skin, black hair, and a swanlike neck—doesn't celebrate violence. Sex is his game. In *Don Juan*, the hero skims and skips from one encounter to the next. His desires are mobile: He can play the woman's part and the man's. Desire doesn't provoke complex ambivalence in Byron, just the need to move from one beckoning satisfaction to the next. Byron's poetry has all the velocity of this ever-moving, ever-changing desire: His rhymes are shrewd, arch, unexpected, and seem to be turned with a wrist flick's ease. Thus Byron on Wordsworth's good friend Samuel Taylor Coleridge, who had just published his *Biographia Literaria*, a book Byron disliked because it was dense and difficult, something you needed to read at least twice: "And Coleridge, too, has lately taken wing, / But like a hawk encumbered with his hood,—/ Explaining metaphysics to the nation—/ I wish he would explain his Explanation."

Byron claimed to compose best on horseback and to be able to concoct dozens of lines in an outing. Wordsworth shouted his lines aloud as he roamed through the Lake District, his dog browsing ahead of him to bark if strangers, who might hear his bellowing and think him mad, appeared on the trail. Byron disliked Wordsworth for one reason above all the rest: boring. The poet of "rocks and stones and trees" was boring. Byron wished never to be bored. So he kept moving, kept accelerating from one point to the next, not in hopes of being satisfied— that he took to be an illusion—but so as not to be overcome by the new-tide demon, ennui. In 1825, the year after Byron died, the first passenger locomotive appeared and maybe, says Camille Paglia, Byron's aristocratic spirit flew by metempsychosis into the machine. Perhaps Byron's restless demon has migrated again, this time from locomotive to laptop.

Students now are quasi-romantics—of a Byronic sort. He would have adored their world of fast travel, fast communication, and fast relationships. There is no more Byronic form of erotic life than the hookup. When after the publication of *Childe Harold's Pilgrimage* Byron became a celebrity—"I awoke and found myself famous," he said—he was surrounded with erotic opportunities. Women sent him notes begging for liaisons;

they followed his carriage through the streets; they smuggled themselves into his rooms. And frequently Byron, who was probably more often seduced than seducing, was pleased to comply. In his superspeed erotic life, Byron is said to have hooked up hundreds of times.

What exactly does it mean to hook up? It means managing to have good sex without activating all the strong feelings that sex usually brings. Hooking up is a fantasy of frictionless sex— sex free of deep emotion. It's sex that lets you keep on sliding over surfaces, moving from partner to partner as smoothly as you move from site to site on the laptop. In fact, the Internet-linked computer is an erotic bazaar, a hookup machine. All of those pages on Facebook are, among other things, personal ads. (Byron would love shopping there—and, more, being shopped for.) Here students (and others, too) can find objects more alluring than pleated skirts. They can find sexual possibilities without end.

Hooking up, of course, is a kind of myth. Sex usually does provoke strong feelings, even when people swear to each other that—this time, this time—it won't. Not everyone is wired like Lord Byron. Students often find that they need continuity and comfort in what can be a harsh college world. Many of them hold faithfully to boyfriends and girlfriends through all four years of school (albeit sometimes with special spring break dispensations). And a few of those students busting out of my class, grabbing for their cell phones, are calling not the alluring near stranger who just texted them, but their parents. In every class I teach, there are at least two or three students who call home every day.

For the way that my students live now is dangerous—some of them know it, some learn in time. "In skating over thin ice,"

Emerson says, "our safety is in our speed." But sometimes, like it or not, we're slowed down or stopped, and then trouble begins. Last term a young woman, an art history and commerce major who was in one of my classes, stopped by my office. She's a marvelous student; I've never taught anyone who could read poetry with much more subtlety and feeling. She was pale, sleepless; her teeth were chattering softly. I invited her to sit down, and then asked some questions. "How many courses are you taking?" Five, no six, seven. "Audits?" Yes, one. "A thesis?" Almost done: She planned to knock out forty pages over the weekend, but now her father, whom she clearly adored, was sick, and she'd have to go home and then how could she—?

"It's too much," I said.

"What?" she hadn't heard me exactly.

"What you're doing? It's too much." And then came—as it almost always does when I say these words, or something like them—a feeling of great relief. Someone with a claim to authority has said that it's okay to be tired, okay to ease up. Okay to rest. When my students crash on their own, they crash like helicopters dropping straight out of the sky when the rotor stops spinning. They're often unaware that they're on the verge of trouble. They're doing what they are supposed to do, what their parents want, with all those courses and the multiple majors; and they haven't got much of any resources to look inside and to see that matters are out of joint—no one has thought to help them acquire those. Did Byron ever fall apart, victim of his own hunger for speed and space? If so, he told us little about it.

I wonder, thinking back, was it something like an encounter I had had—to take the reincarnation trope a step further—with Lord Byron that fall day on the Lawn? He was all for glamour and motion. I was all for—well, what was I for? Was it the magic of the fifth draft on a project about a thinker, Freud, about whom—let us be generous—not everyone seems to care a great deal? I admit that I love that line of Yeats's about how writing is ceaseless stitching and unstitching, but "if it does not seem a moment's thought / Our stitching and unstitching has been naught." The stitching-unstitching business fascinates me. Yet my student had been to six countries, *six!*—and that was only part of his summer's story. If you asked returning students now for that old composition standard—What I Did This Summer—they'd have to hit you with three-decker novels.

And what do I have to offer the speedsters, I, a slow person from the generation of one kind of Coke, three TV stations, one mom and one dad? How exactly do we professors teach this kind of student? What do they need to know?

Many of my colleagues have a ready answer, and its essence is this: If you can't lick 'em, join 'em. In effect, they've made the courses an extension of the Internet. Their classes are laser and light shows, fast-moving productions that mime the colors and sound and above all the velocity of the laptop. There are movie screens, sound systems, Internet tie-ins. And, these colleagues say, it works. One professor I know equips his students with handheld wireless input devices that have twelve buttons and look a lot like TV remotes. Every five minutes or so he stops teaching and polls the kids to see how well they're doing. I admire the resourcefulness that's on display here—and I admire the skill and energy that many of my fellow teachers have deployed to meet students halfway. And yet . . .

Not long ago, a younger colleague came by my office to chat and at a certain point informed me that her son, who was four years old, had a favorite dinosaur and that it was called the Edmontosaurus. ("Edmundosaurus" is what I could have sworn she said.) She remarked, with what seemed untainted goodwill, that this may be the very oldest of the dinosaurs. A few weeks later she came by again—was she wheeling a TV in front of her, taking it to class?—and ended up telling me about this Edmundosaurus one more time. Well, the kind of schooling I endorse goes back at least as far as Socrates and maybe further, though—thanks anyway for the suggestion—not all the way to the thunder lizards.

For a student to be educated, she has to face brilliant antagonists: She has to encounter thinkers who see the world in different terms than she does. Does she come to college as a fundamentalist guardian of crude faith? Then two necessary books for her are Freud's *Future of an Illusion* and Nietzsche's *The Anti-Christ*. Once she's weathered the surface insults, she may find herself in an intellectual version of paradise, where she can defend her beliefs or change them, and where what's on hand is not a chance conversation, as Socrates liked to say, but a dialogue about how to live.

Is the student a scion of high-minded liberals who think that religion is the Oxycontin—the redneck heroin—of Redneck Nation? Then on might come William James and *The Varieties of Religious Experience* or Schopenhauer's essays on faith. It's this kind of dialogue, deliberate, gradual, thoughtful, that students immersed in the manic culture of Internet and Adderall are conditioned not to have. The first step for the professor now is to slow his classroom down. The common phrase for what he wants to do is telling: We "stop and think." Stop. Our students rarely get a chance to stop: They're always in motion, always spitting out what comes first to mind, never challenging, checking, revising.

Not long ago a young man came to my office, plopped down, and looked at me with tired urgency. "Give me ten minutes on Freud," he said. "Convince me that he really has something important to tell me." Despite appearances, this was a good moment. It was a chance to try to persuade him to slow it down. Get one of Freud's books—*Civilization and Its Discontents* is usually the best place to start—read it once and again, then come back for a talk.

When you have that kind of conversation, one on one, you begin, however modestly, to create a university. Why does the encounter need to take place face-to-face, rather than online? Because the student and teacher need to create a bond of good feeling, where they are free to speak openly with each other. They need to connect not just through cold print but through gestures, intonations, jokes. The student needs to discover what the teacher knows and what she exemplifies about how to live; the teacher needs contact with the student's energy and hopes. That kind of connection happens best in person; perhaps it can only happen that way.

This Socratic education, the goal of which is self-knowledge, is not a luxury. Over years of teaching I have seen that those students who, through whatever form of struggle, really have come to an independent sense of who they are and what they want are the ones who genuinely thrive in the world. Thoreau says that if you advance in the direction of your dreams, you'll find uncommon success, and teaching a few generations of students has persuaded me that he is right. The ones who do what they love without a lot of regard for conventional success tend to turn out happy and strong.

We teachers need to remind ourselves from time to time that our primary job is not to help our students to acquire skills, marketable skills, bankables. And we don't preeminently teach communication and computation and instill habits of punctuality and thoroughness. We're not here to help our students make their minds resemble their laptops, fast and feverish. We didn't get into teaching to make trains of thought run on time.

As for our students, all honor to them: They may have something to teach the five-drafter. By their hunger for more life, they convey hope that the world is still a splendid place, worth seeing and appreciating. Into spontaneity they can liberate us. But life is more than spontaneity and whim. (To live well, we must sometimes stop and think and then try to remake the work in progress that we currently are. There's no better place for that than a college classroom where, together, we can slow it down and live deliberately.)

And to that end (Edmundosaurus, take the microphone): No more laptops in my classroom. You can leave them at home. You can check 'em at the door.

FELLOW STUDENTS

WHO ARE YOU AND WHAT ARE YOU DOING HERE?
A Word to the Incoming Class

WELCOME AND CONGRATULATIONS: Getting to the first day of college is a major achievement. You're to be commended, and not just you, but the parents, grandparents, uncles, and aunts who helped get you here.

It's been said that raising a child effectively takes a village: Well, as you may have noticed, our American village is not in very good shape. We've got guns, drugs, wars, fanatical religions, a slime-based popular culture, and some politicians who—a little restraint here—aren't what they might be. Merely to survive in this American village and to win a place in the entering class has taken a lot of grit on your part. So, yes, congratulations to all.

You now may think that you've about got it made. Amid the impressive college buildings, in company with a high-powered faculty, surrounded by the best of your generation, all you need is to keep doing what you've done before: Work hard, get good grades, listen to your teachers, get along with the people around you, and you'll emerge in four years as an educated young man or woman. Ready for life.

Do not believe it. It is not true. If you want to get a real education in America, you're going to have to fight—and I don't mean just fight against the drugs and the violence and against the slime-based culture that is still going to surround you. I mean something a little more disturbing. To get an education, you're probably going to have to fight against the institution that you find yourself in—no matter how prestigious it may be. (In fact, the more prestigious the school, the more you'll probably have to push.) You can get a terrific education in America now—there are astonishing opportunities at almost every college—but the education will not be presented to you wrapped and bowed. To get it, you'll need to struggle and strive, to be strong, and occasionally even to piss off some admirable people.

I came to college with few resources, but one of them was an understanding, however crude, of how I might use my opportunities there. This I began to develop because of my father, who had never been to college—in fact, he'd barely gotten out of high school. One night after dinner, he and I were sitting in our kitchen at 58 Clewley Road in Medford, Massachusetts, hatching plans about the rest of my life. I was about to go off to college, a feat no one in my family had accomplished in living memory. "I think I might want to be prelaw," I told my father. I had no idea what being prelaw was. My father compressed his brow and blew twin streams of smoke, dragonlike, from his magnificent nose. "Do you want to be a lawyer?" he asked. My father had some experience with lawyers, and with policemen, too; he was not well disposed toward either. "I'm not really sure," I told him, "but lawyers make pretty good money, right?"

My father detonated. (That was not uncommon. He detonated a lot.) He told me that I was going to go to college only once, and that while I was there I had better study what I wanted. He said that when rich kids went to school, they majored in the subjects that interested them, and that my younger brother Philip and I were as good as any rich kids. (We were rich kids minus the money.) Wasn't I interested in literature? I confessed that I was. Then I had better study literature, unless I had inside information to the effect that reincarnation wasn't just hype, and I'd be able to attend college thirty or forty times. If I had such info, prelaw would be fine, and maybe even a tour through invertebrate biology could also be tossed in. But until I had the reincarnation stuff from a solid source, I better get to work and pick out some English classes from the course catalog.

"How about the science requirements?" I asked.

"Take 'em later," he said. "You never know."

My father, Wright Aukenhead Edmundson, Malden High School class of 1948 (by a hair), knew the score. What he told me that evening at the Clewley Road kitchen table was true in itself, and it also contains the germ of an idea about what a university education should be. But apparently almost everyone else—students, teachers, trustees, and parents—see the matter much differently. They have it wrong.

Education has one salient enemy in present-day America, and that enemy is education—university education in particular. To almost everyone, university education is a means to an end. For students, that end is a good job. Students want the credentials that will help them get ahead. They want the certificate that will grant them access to Wall Street, or entrance into law or medical or business school. And how can we blame them? America values power and money, big players with big bucks. When we raise our children, we tell them in multiple ways that what we want most for them is success—material success. To be poor in America is to be a failure. It's to be without decent health care, without basic necessities, often without dignity. Then there are those backbreaking student loans: People leave school as servants, indentured to pay massive bills, so that first job better be a good one. Students come to college with the goal of a diploma in mind—what happens to them in between, especially in classrooms, is often of no deep and determining interest to them.

In college, life is elsewhere. Life is at parties, at clubs, in music, with friends, in sports. Life is what celebrities have. The idea that the courses you take should be the primary objective of going to college is tacitly considered absurd. In terms of their work, students live in the future and not the present; they live with their prospects for success. If universities stopped issuing credentials, half of the clients would be gone by tomorrow morning, with the remainder following fast behind.

The faculty, too, is often absent: Their real lives are also elsewhere. Like most of their students, they aim to get on. The work they are compelled to do to advance—get tenure, promotion, raises, outside offers—is, broadly speaking, scholarly work. No matter what anyone says, this work has precious little to do with the fundamentals of teaching. The proof is that virtually no undergraduate students can read and understand their professors' scholarly publications. The public senses this disparity and so thinks of the professors' work as being silly or beside the point. Some of it is. But the public also senses that because professors don't pay full-bore attention to teaching, they don't have to work very hard—they've created a massive feather bed for themselves and called it a university.

This is radically false. Ambitious professors, the ones who, like their students, want to get ahead in America, work furiously. Scholarship, even if pretentious and almost unreadable, is nonetheless labor-intense. One can slave for a year or two on a single article for publication in this or that refereed journal. These essays are honest: Their footnotes reflect real reading, real assimilation, and real dedication. Shoddy work—in which the author cheats, cuts corners, copies from others—is quickly detected. The people who do the work have highly developed intellectual powers, and they push themselves hard to reach a certain standard. That the results have almost no practical relevance for students, the public, or even, frequently, other scholars is a central element in the tragicomedy that is often academia.

The students and the professors have made a deal: Neither of them has to throw himself heart and soul into what happens in the classroom. The students write their abstract, overintellectualized essays; the professors grade the students for their capacity to be abstract and overintellectual—and often genuinely smart. For their essays can be brilliant, in a chilly way; they can also be clipped from the Internet, and often are. Whatever the case, no one wants to invest too much in them—for life is elsewhere. The professor saves his energies for the profession, while the student saves his for friends, social life, volunteer work, making connections, and getting in position to clasp hands on the true grail, the first job.

No one in this picture is evil; no one is criminally irresponsible. It's just that smart people are prone to look into matters to see how they might go about buttering their toast. Then they butter their toast.

As for the administrators, their relation to the students often seems based not on love but fear. Administrators fear bad publicity, scandal, and dissatisfaction on the part of their customers.

More than anything else, though, they fear lawsuits. Throwing a student out of college for this or that piece of bad behavior is very difficult, almost impossible. The student will sue your eyes out. One kid I knew (and rather liked) threatened on his blog to mince his dear and esteemed professor (me) with a samurai sword for the crime of having taught a boring class. (The class *was* a little boring—I had a damn cold—but the punishment seemed a bit severe.) The dean of students laughed lightly when I suggested that this behavior might be grounds for sending the student on a brief vacation. I was, you might say, discomfited, and showed up to class for a while with my cell phone jiggered to dial 911 with one touch.

Still, this was small potatoes. Colleges are even leery of disciplining guys who have committed sexual assault, or assault plain and simple. Instead of being punished, these guys frequently stay around, strolling the quad and swilling the libations, an affront (and sometimes a terror) to their victims.

You'll find that cheating is common as well. As far as I can discern, the student ethos goes like this: If the professor is so lazy that he gives the same test every year, it's okay to go ahead and take advantage—you've got better things to do. The Internet is amok with services selling term papers, and those services exist, capitalism being what it is, because people purchase the papers—lots of them. Fraternity files bulge with old tests from a variety of courses. Periodically, the public gets exercised about this situation and there are articles in the national news. But then interest dwindles and matters go back to normal.

One of the reasons professors sometimes look the other way when they sense cheating is that it sends them into a world of sorrow. A friend of mine had the temerity to detect cheating on the part of a kid who was the nephew of a well-placed official in an Arab government complexly aligned with the U.S. Black limousines pulled up in front of his office and disgorged decorously suited negotiators. Did my pal fold? No, he's not the type. But he did not enjoy the process.

What colleges generally want are well-rounded students, civic leaders, people who know what the system demands, how to keep matters light and not push too hard for an education or anything else; people who get their credentials and leave professors alone to do their brilliant work so they may rise and enhance the rankings of the university. Such students leave and become donors and so, in their own turn, contribute immeasurably to the university's standing. They've done a fine job skating on surfaces in high school—the best way to get an across-the-board outstanding record—and now they're on campus to cut a few more figure eights.

In a culture where the major and determining values are monetary, what else could you do? How else would you live if not by getting all you can, succeeding all you can, making all you can?

The idea that a university education really should have no substantial content, should not be about what John Keats was disposed to call "Soul-making," is one that you might think professors and university presidents would be discreet about. Not so. This view informed an address that Richard Brodhead gave to the senior class at Yale before he departed to become president of Duke. Brodhead, an impressive, articulate man, seems to take as his educational touchstone the Duke of Wellington's precept that the Battle of Waterloo was won on the playing fields of Eton. Brodhead suggests that the content of the course isn't really what matters. In five years (or five months, or minutes), the student is likely to have forgotten how to do the problem sets and will only hazily recollect what happens in the ninth book of *Paradise Lost*. The legacy of their college years will be a legacy of difficulties overcome. When they face equally arduous tasks later in life, students will tap their old resources of determination, and they'll win.

All right, there's nothing wrong with this as far as it goes—after all, the student who writes a brilliant forty-page thesis in a hard week has learned more than a little about her inner resources. Maybe it will give her needed confidence in the future. But doesn't the content of the courses matter at all?

On the evidence of this talk, no. Trying to figure out whether the stuff you're reading is true or false and being open to having your life changed is a fraught, controversial activity. Doing so requires energy from the professor—which is better spent on other matters. This kind of perspective-altering teaching and learning can cause the things that administrators fear above all else: trouble, arguments, bad press, et cetera. After the kid-samurai episode, the chair of my department not unsympathetically suggested that this was the sort of incident that could happen when you brought a certain intensity to teaching. At the time I found this remark a tad detached, but maybe he was right.

So if you want an education, the odds aren't with you: The professors are off doing what they call their own work; the other students, who've doped out the way the place runs, are busy leaving their professors alone and getting themselves in position for bright and shining futures; the student-services people are trying to keep everyone content, offering plenty of entertainment and building another state-of-the-art workout facility every few months. The development office is already scanning you for future donations.

So why make trouble? Why not just go along? Let the profs roam free in the realms of pure thought, let yourselves party in the realms of impure pleasure, and let the student-services gang assert fewer prohibitions and newer delights for you. You'll get a good job, you'll have plenty of friends, you'll have a driveway of your own.

You'll also, if my father and I are right, be truly and righteously screwed. The reason for this is simple. The quest at the center of a liberal arts education is not a luxury quest; it's a necessity quest. If you do not undertake it, you risk leading a life of desperation—maybe quiet; maybe, in time, very loud—and I am not exaggerating. For you risk trying to be someone other than who you are, which, in the long run, is killing.

By the time you come to college, you will have been told who you are numberless times. Your parents and friends, your teachers, your counselors, your priests and rabbis and ministers and imams have all had their say. They've let you know how they size you up, and they've let you know what they think you should value. They've given you a sharp and protracted taste of what they feel is good and bad, right and wrong. Much is on their side. They have confronted you with scriptures—holy books that, whatever their actual provenance, have given people what they feel to be wisdom for thousands of years. They've given you family traditions—you've learned the ways of your tribe and community. And, too, you've been tested, probed, looked at up and down and through. The coach knows what your athletic prospects are, the guidance office has a sheaf of test scores that relegate you to this or that ability quadrant, and your teachers have got you pegged. You are, as Foucault might say, the intersection of many evaluative and potentially determining discourses: You, boy, you, girl, have been made.

And—contra Foucault—that's not so bad. Embedded in all of the major religions are profound truths. Schopenhauer, who despised belief in transcendent things, nonetheless taught Christianity to be of inexpressible worth. He couldn't believe in the divinity of Jesus or in the afterlife, but to Schopenhauer, a deep pessimist, a religion that had as its central emblem the figure of a man being tortured on a cross couldn't be entirely misleading. To the Christian, Schopenhauer said, pain was at the center of the understanding of life, and that was just as it should be.

One does not need to be as harsh as Schopenhauer to understand the use of religion, even if one does not believe in an otherworldly God. And all those teachers and counselors and friends—and the prognosticating uncles, the dithering aunts, the fathers and mothers with their hopes for your fulfillment, or their fulfillment in you—should not necessarily be cast aside or ignored. Families have their wisdom. The question "Who do they think you are at home?" is never an idle one.

The major conservative thinkers have always been very serious about what goes by the name of common sense. Edmund Burke saw common sense as a loosely made but often profound collective work in which humanity deposited its hard-earned wisdom—the precipitate of joy and tears—over time. You have been raised in proximity to common sense, if you've been raised at all, and common sense is something to respect, though not quite—peace unto the formidable Burke—to revere.

You may be all that the good people who raised you say you are; you may want all they have shown you is worth wanting; you may be someone who is truly your father's son or your mother's daughter. But then again, you may not be.

For the power that is in you, as Emerson suggested, may be

new in nature. You may not be the person that your parents take you to be. And—this thought is both more exciting and more dangerous—you may not be the person that you take yourself to be, either. You may not have read yourself aright, and college is the place where you can find out whether you have or not. The reason to read Blake and Dickinson and Freud and Dickens is not to become more cultivated or more articulate or to be someone who, at a cocktail party, is never embarrassed (or can embarrass others). The best reason to read them is to see if they know you better than you know yourself. You may find your own suppressed and rejected thoughts following back to you with an "alienated majesty." Reading the great writers, you may have the experience Longinus associated with the sublime: You feel that you have actually created the text yourself. For somehow your predecessors are more yourself than you are.

This was my own experience reading the two writers who have influenced me the most, Sigmund Freud and Ralph Waldo Emerson. They gave words to thoughts and feelings that I had never been able to render myself. They shone a light onto the world, and what they saw, suddenly I saw, too. From Emerson I learned to trust my own thoughts, to trust them even when every voice seems to be on the other side. I need the wherewithal, as Emerson did, to say what's on my mind and to take the inevitable hits. Much more I learned from the sage—about character, about loss, about joy, about writing and its secret sources, but Emerson most centrally preaches the gospel of self-reliance, and that is what I have tried most to take from him. I continue to hold in mind one of Emerson's most memorable passages: "Society is a joint-stock company, in which the members agree, for the better securing of his bread to each shareholder, to surrender the liberty and culture of the eater. The virtue in most request is conformity. Self-reliance is its aversion. It loves not realities and creators, but names and customs."

Emerson's greatness lies not only in showing you how powerful names and customs can be, but also in demonstrating how exhilarating it is to buck them. When he came to Harvard to talk about religion, he shocked the professors and students by challenging the divinity of Jesus and the truth of his miracles. He wasn't invited back for decades.

From Freud I found a great deal to ponder as well. I don't mean Freud the aspiring scientist, but the Freud who was a speculative essayist and interpreter of the human condition like Emerson. Freud challenges nearly every significant human ideal. He goes after religion. He says that it comes down to the longing for the father. He goes after love. He calls it "the overestimation of the erotic object." He attacks our desire for charismatic popular leaders. We're drawn to them because we hunger for absolute authority. He declares that dreams don't predict the future and that there's nothing benevolent about them. They're disguised fulfillments of repressed wishes.

Freud has something challenging and provoking to say about virtually every human aspiration. I learned that if I wanted to affirm any consequential ideal, I had to talk my way past Freud. He was—and is—a perpetual challenge and goad.

Never has there been a more shrewd and imaginative cartographer of the psyche. His separation of the self into three parts, and his sense of the fraught, anxious, but often negotiable relations among them (negotiable when you come to the game with a Freudian knowledge), does a great deal to help one navigate experience. (Though sometimes—and I owe this to Emerson—it seems right to let the psyche fall into civil war, accepting barrages of anxiety and grief for this or that good reason.)

The battle is to make such writers one's own, to winnow them out and to find their essential truths. We need to see where they fall short and where they exceed the mark, and then to develop them a little, as the ideas themselves, one comes to see, actually developed others. (Both Emerson and Freud live out of Shakespeare—but only a giant can be truly influenced by Shakespeare.) In reading, I continue to look for one thing—to be influenced, to learn something new, to be thrown off my course and onto another, better way.

My father knew that he was dissatisfied with life. He knew that none of the descriptions people had for him quite fit. He understood that he was always out of joint with life as it was. He had talent: My brother and I each got about half the raw ability he possessed, and that's taken us through life well enough. But what to do with that talent—there was the rub for my father. He used to stroll through the house intoning his favorite line from Groucho Marx's ditty "Whatever It Is, I'm Against It." (I recently asked my son, now twenty-one, if he thought I was mistaken in teaching him this particular song when he was six years old. "No!" he said, filling the air with an invisible forest of exclamation points.) But what my father never managed to get was a sense of who he might become. He never had a world of possibilities spread before him, never made sustained contact with the best that has been thought and said. He didn't get to revise his understanding of himself, figure out what he'd do best that might give the world some profit.

My father was a gruff man but also a generous one, so that night at the kitchen table at 58 Clewley Road he made an effort to let me have the chance that had been denied to him by both fate and character. He gave me the chance to see what I was all about, and if it proved to be different from him, proved even to be something he didn't like or entirely comprehend, then he'd deal with it.

Right now, if you're going to get a real education, you may have to be aggressive and assertive.

Your professors will give you some fine books to read, and they'll probably help you understand them. What they won't do, for reasons that perplex me, is ask you if the books contain truths you could live your life by. When you read Plato, you'll probably learn about his metaphysics and his politics and his way of conceiving the soul. But no one will ask you if his ideas are good enough to believe in. No one will ask you, in the words of Emerson's disciple William James, what their "cash value" might be. No one will suggest that you might use Plato as your bible for a week or a year or longer. No one, in short, will ask you to use Plato to help you change your life.

That will be up to you. You must put the question of Plato to yourself. You must ask whether reason should always rule the passions, philosophers should always rule the state, and poets should inevitably be banished from a just commonwealth. You have to ask yourself if wildly expressive music (rock and rap and the rest) deranges the soul in ways that are destructive to its health. You must inquire of yourself if balanced calm is the most desirable human state.

Occasionally—for you will need some help in fleshing out the answers—you may have to prod your professors to see if they will take the text at hand—in this case the divine and disturbing Plato—to be true. And you will have to be tough if the professor mocks you for uttering a sincere question instead of keeping matters easy for all concerned by staying detached and analytical. (Detached analysis has a place, but in the end you've got to speak from the heart and pose the question of truth.) You'll be the one who pesters your teachers. You'll ask your history teacher about whether there is a design to our history, whether we're progressing or declining, or whether, in the words of a fine recent play, *The History Boys*, history's "just one fuckin' thing after another." You'll be the one who challenges your biology teacher about the intellectual conflict between evolutionist and creationist thinking. You'll not only question the statistics teacher about what numbers *can* explain but what they can't.

Because every subject you study is a language, and since you may adopt one of these languages as your own, you'll want to know how to speak it expertly and also how it fails to deal with those concerns for which it has no adequate words. You'll be looking into the reach of every metaphor that every discipline offers, and you'll be trying to see around their corners.

The whole business is scary, of course. What if you arrive at college devoted to premed, sure that nothing will make you and your family happier than life as a physician, only to discover that elementary schoolteaching is where your heart is?

You might learn that you're not meant to be a doctor at all. Of course, given your intellect and discipline, you can still probably be one. You can pound your round peg through the very square hole of medical school, then go off into the profession. And society will help you. Society has a cornucopia of resources to encourage you in doing what society needs done but that you don't much like doing and are not cut out to do.

To ease your grief, society offers alcohol, television, drugs, divorce, and buying, buying, buying what you don't need. But all those, too, have their costs.

Education is about finding out what form of work for you is close to being play—work you do so easily that it restores you as you go. Randall Jarrell once said that if he were a rich man, he would pay money to teach poetry to students. (I would, too, for what it's worth.) In saying that, he (like my father) hinted in the direction of a profound and true theory of learning.

Having found what's best for you to do, you may be surprised by how far you rise, how prosperous, even against your own projections, you become. The student who eschews medical school to follow his gift for teaching small children spends his twenties in low-paying but pleasurable and soul-rewarding toil. He's always behind on his student-loan payments; he still lives in a house with four other guys, not all of whom got proper instructions on how to clean a bathroom. He buys shirts from the Salvation Army, has intermittent Internet, and vacations where he can. But lo—he has a gift for teaching. He writes an essay about how to teach, then a book—which no one buys. But he writes another—in part out of a feeling of injured merit, perhaps—and that one they do buy.

Money is still a problem, but in a new sense. The world wants him to write more, lecture, travel more, and will pay him for his efforts, and he likes this a good deal. But he also likes staying around and showing up at school and figuring out how to get this or that little runny-nosed specimen to begin learning how to read. These are the kinds of problems that are worth having, and if you advance, as Thoreau asked us to do, in the general direction of your dreams, you may have them. If you advance in the direction of someone else's dreams—if you want to live someone else's dreams rather than yours—then get a TV for every room, buy yourself a lifetime supply of your favorite quaff, crank up the porn channel, and groove away. But when we expend our energies in rightful ways, Robert Frost observed, we stay whole and vigorous and we don't get weary. "Strongly spent," the poet says, "is synonymous with kept."

DO SPORTS BUILD CHARACTER?

T HE FIRST YEAR I played high school football, the coaches were united in their belief that drinking water on the practice field was dangerous. It made you cramp up, they told us. It made you sick to your stomach, they said. So during practice, which went on for two and a half hours, twice a day, during a roaring New England summer, we got no water. Players cramped up anyway; players got sick to their stomachs regardless. Players fell on their knees and began making soft plaintive noises; they were helped to their feet, escorted to the locker room, and seen no more. On the first day of double sessions, there were about 120 players—tough Irish and Italian kids and a few blacks—and by the end of the twelve-day ordeal there were sixty left. Some of us began without proper equipment. I started without cleats. But this was not a problem: Soon someone who wore your size shoes or shoulder pads would quit, and then you could have theirs.

The coaches didn't cut anyone from my high school squad that year. Kids cut themselves. Guys with what appeared to me to be spectacular athletic talent would, after four days of double-session drills, walk hangdog into the coaches' locker room and hand over their pads. The coaches rarely tried to encourage them to stay. If a kid couldn't take it, he couldn't take it. There was no water and there were no compassionate paternal talks. There were the two-and-a-half-hour practices twice a day; each of which ended with grass drills. We formed ranks and ran in place; when the coach blew the whistle, we jumped up, spread-eagled ourselves in the air, and went bang onto the hard ground. Then we got up and started running in place again. Some guys went bang and stayed down on the deck panting, which meant that they needed to quit. They brought their dirty practice gear home, got it washed by their mothers, and presented it in a white, fresh-smelling bundle, like a fluffy loaf of home-baked bread, to the coaches the next morning. When I asked one of them why he quit, he said simply, "I couldn't take it."

Could I? There was no reason going in to think that I would be able to. I was buttery soft around the waist, nearsighted, not especially fast, and not quick at all. It turned out that underneath the soft exterior I had some muscle and that my lung capacity was well developed, probably from vicious bouts of asthma I'd had as a boy, when I'd fought for air as hard as any marathon runner, perhaps harder. (The marathon runner has the luxury of stepping out of the race; not the asthmatic.) But compared to my fellow ballplayers, my physical gifts were meager. What I had was a will that was anything but weak. It was a surprise to me, and to everyone who knew me, how ferociously I wanted to stay with the game.

Still, things did not look promising. Sometimes after morning practice I was so dazed that it took me an hour to shower and get dressed. By the time I was in my street clothes, the locker room was usually empty. Sometimes I wasn't sure that I would be able to find my way to the bus stop and get home, so I went below the bleachers and fell asleep, woke up two hours later, hiked to a convenience store to buy what passed for a lunch, and then went to sleep under the stands again. By four o'clock, when the other players were returning, I was in front of my locker and dressing in slow motion. In an hour I was on the field, ready to go. I cried in my sleep once at the thought that the next day I would have to go back to practice. But I went. I didn't miss a day, didn't fake an injury, didn't duck a drill, and at the end of double sessions—a shock to myself—I was a ballplayer.

Did I love the game? I surely liked it. I liked how when I was deep in fatigue, I became a tougher, more daring person, even a reckless one. One night, scrimmaging, I went head-on with the star running back, a guy who outweighed me by twenty pounds and was far faster and stronger. I did what the coaches said: I squared up, got low (in football, the answer to every difficulty is to get low, or get lower), and planted him. I did that? I asked myself. Me? I liked being the guy who could do that—sometimes, though alas, not often enough. The intensity of the game was an inebriate. It conquered my grinding self-consciousness, brought me out of myself.

I liked the transforming aspect of the game: I came to the field one thing, a diffident guy with a slack body, and I worked like a dog and so became something else, a guy with some physical prowess and a touch more faith in himself. Mostly I suppose I liked the whole process because it was so damn hard. I didn't think I could make it and no one I knew did either. I knew that my parents were ready to console me if I came home bruised and dead weary and said that I was quitting. In time, one of the coaches confessed to me that he was sure I'd be gone in a few days. I had not succeeded in anything for a long time: I was a crappy student; socially I was close to a wash; my part-time job was scrubbing pans in a hospital kitchen; the first girl I liked in high school didn't like me; the second and the third jumped in behind and followed her lead. But football was something I could do, or at least do halfway. (I was never going to be anything like a star.) It was hard and it took some strength of will and—clumsily, passionately—I could do it.

"Long live what I badly did at Clemson," James Dickey says in "The Bee," the poem about his football days at college. Dickey wasn't much of a player, either, it seems. He remembers his inept lunges into the line and recalls the coaches badgering him, not unlike the way they badgered me: " 'God damn you Dickey, *dig!* ' " The old coaches have come back to Dickey years later, when he's afflicted by the malaise of middle age. They holler at him to get the lead out and to sprint for all he's worth into the midst of ferocious California freeway traffic, where his son, stung by a bee and terrified, has blindly run. Dickey digs. He leaves his feet—the ballplayer's most desperate maneuver. He makes it. "I have him where / He lives," the poet says, "and down we go singing with screams into / The dirt." And the screams of the coaches turn, finally, into whispers of approval. Dead coaches, like Shag Norton, Dickey's backfield coach, live in the air, the poet tells his son; they live in the ear. They want you better than you are. They scream at you when something must be saved.

I understand, I think. Though I never had much overt

affection for the coaches (or they for me), I knew that the objective of the game on the deepest level wasn't to score touchdowns or make tackles or to block kicks. The game was much more about practice than about the Saturday-afternoon contests themselves. And practice was about trying to do something over and over again and failing and failing and then finally succeeding partway. Practice was about showing up and doing the same drills day after day and getting stronger and faster by tiny, tiny increments and then discovering that by the end of the season you were effectively another person. But mostly football was about those first days of double sessions when everyone who stuck with it did something he imagined was impossible and so learned to recalibrate his instruments. In the future what immediately looked impossible to us—what said Back Off, Not for You—had to be looked at again and maybe attempted anyway. We'd already done something we thought we couldn't: Maybe this next citadel would fall, this next granite block would give way to shape and proportion, with a dose, maybe a double dose, of the effort we'd applied on that miserable unyielding field under the sun that turned your helmet into a boiling cauldron and your brain—truly, it sometimes felt this way—into simmering mush.

When we seemed to get hurt on the field, when we went down and didn't immediately get up, the coaches had a common reaction: "Get up and walk it off." Sometimes, granted, the stretcher had to come out, but not often. It was surprising how many times it was possible to rise like Lazarus after a collision that felt like a couple of bowling balls rolling together. I once tried to tackle a tight end who was six inches taller and fifty pounds heavier than I was. I bounced off and hit the so-called turf so hard that I felt the fillings in the back of my mouth jump; I passed out for an instant and woke up thinking my back was broken. "Get up. Walk it off. You're all right." I did and I was.

Tim Green, the onetime star defensive end for the Atlanta Falcons, makes a point about playing ball, a point that carries over into other areas of experience. There's one factor at the heart of the game, he says. And that is you have to get up. You get smacked around and knocked to the ground on at least half the plays, but then you have to get up. You have to rise and go on to the next play. "I am defeated all the time," says Emerson, "yet to victory I am born." Football demonstrates that one is defeated, knocked down, time after time, and it also shows that victory is an uncertain thing, whether you think you're born to it or not.

Speaking for myself, I've never had to call on the spirit of grass drills or double sessions or channel an old coach in order to save myself or a child—there's never been that drastic a moment. (Lord defend me from such.) But I do recall what it felt like when, having thrown all I thought I had into writing a chunk of my dissertation, I came back from the job market a complete flop. I had come in with hopes that pointed to the heights: I didn't want merely any academic job, though at the time that would have been hard enough. I wanted one of the dozen or so best ones that every year had about four hundred applicants apiece. If I couldn't get one, I decided, I'd quit and do something else. After the grand belly flop—like a grass drill drop, with no control—I knew that I'd have to work on a level higher by far than I had on anything I'd ever approached. I'd coasted at my ease through grad school, or so it now seemed. So I began living in the library, much in the way that I lived at the football stadium my first summer on the team, arriving in the stacks early, leaving only to go to the gym in the late afternoon and to eat dinner, then returning until past dark. I built a wall of books on my table as though to cloister myself in like a medieval monk. Did I call on the old spirit of double sessions? Quietly, pretty quietly, I did. I kept it largely to myself, since most scholars don't see much symmetry between what they do and what runners and jumpers and (especially) blockers and tacklers attempt. I read every book in the library on John Keats, the subject of my first chapter, and most of the articles. I wrote and rewrote my first paragraph about thirty times—like those grass drills, over and over and over again. When the summer was through I had a chapter I could be proud of and that I knew would take me where I wanted to go.

Doctoral dissertations are tougher than one might imagine: It's lonely work and no one (sometimes least of all your dissertation advisor, who has other things to do) cares much if you flourish or pucker on the vine. But compared to what others are compelled to endure—severe illness, divorce, the mortal sickness of a child—sitting in an air-conditioned library trying to make sense out of the way other people have tried to make sense of the world isn't all that daunting. But others, I know, have called on their experience in sports to summon larger doses of courage. They've used their old sports experience as a map to take them back to their reserves of strength they had forgotten they possessed. "Diversity of strength will attend us," the poet says, "if but once we have been strong." For many of us, the time of being strong was the time we played a sport. Do sports build character? Of course they do. Who could doubt it?

Sports are many things, but one of the things they are is an imitation of heroic culture. They mimic the martial world; they fabricate the condition of war. (Boxing doesn't fabricate war; it *is* war and, to my mind, not a sport. As Joyce Carol Oates says, you play football and baseball and basketball. No one "plays" boxing.) This fabrication is in many ways a good thing— necessary to the health of a society. For it seems to me that Plato is right and that the desire for glory is part of everyone's spirit. Plato called this desire *thymos,* and he associated its ascendancy and celebration with Homer. The objective of his great work, *The Republic,* is to show how for a civilization to truly thrive, it must find a way to make the drive for glory subordinate to reason. Plato believes that war is sometimes necessary, but that going to war should be up to the rulers, the philosopher kings, who have developed their minds fully. Some of us, Plato says, have a hunger for martial renown that surpasses others', and those people are very valuable and very dangerous. They need praise when they fight well (for material rewards don't mean much to them), and they need something to keep them occu- pied when no war is at hand. Sport is a way to do this. Plato would probably approve of the way athletics function in our culture—they let the most thymotic of us express the hunger for conquest, and they allow the rest of us to get our hit of glory through identification.

But there are warriors and there are *warriors*; there are ath- letes and there are *athletes*. In the Western heroic tradition, the paragon of the humane warrior is Homer's Hector, prince of the Trojans. He is a fierce fighter: On one particular day, no Greek can stand up to him; his valor puts the whole Greek army to route. Even on an unexceptional day, Hector can stand against Ajax, the Greek giant, and trade blow for blow with him. Yet as fierce as Hector can be, he is also humane. He is a loving son to his aged parents, a husband who talks on equal terms with his wife, Andromache, and he is a tenderhearted father. He and King Priam, his own father, are the only ones in Troy who treat Helen, the ostensible cause of the war, with kindness. One of the most memorable scenes in *The Iliad* comes when Hector strides toward his boy, Astyanax, coming fresh from the battlefield. The child screams with fright at the ferocious form, encased in armor, covered with dust and gore. Hector understands his child in an instant and takes off his helmet, with its giant horsehair plume, then bends over, picks his boy up, and dandles him while Andromache looks on happily. Astyanax—who will soon be pitched from off the battlements of Troy when the Greeks conquer the city—stares up at his father and laughs.

The scene concentrates what is most appealing about Hector—and about a certain kind of athlete and warrior. Hector can turn it off. He can stop being the manslayer that he needs to be out there on the windy plains of Troy and become a humane husband and father. The scene shows him in his dual nature—warrior and man of thought and feeling. In a sense, he is the figure that every fighter and everyone who takes the athletic field should aspire to emulate. He is the Navy Seal or the Green Beret who would never kill a prisoner; the fearless fighter who could never harm a woman or a child. In the symbolic world of sports, where the horrors and the triumphs of combat are only mimicked, he is the one who comports himself with extreme gentleness off the field, who never speaks ill of an opponent, who never complains, never whines. The dual nature of the noble athlete finds a concentrated image in football: When the play starts, the player goes all out, takes chances, is reckless; when the whistle blows, he becomes his civilized self again, doesn't argue or complain, but walks with dignity back to his huddle. Plato greatly admired people who, though possessed with strong will, could still use their reason and their fellow feeling to temper themselves.

But *The Iliad* is not primarily about Hector. It is the poem of Achilles and his wrath. After Hector kills Achilles' dear friend Patroclus, Achilles goes on a rampage, killing every Trojan he can. All humanity leaves him; all mercy is gone. At one point, a Trojan fighter grasps his knees and begs for mercy. Achilles taunts him. Look at me, he says, so strong and beautiful, and someday I too shall have to die. But not today. Today is your day. At one point a river close to the city, the River Scamander, becomes incensed over Achilles' murdering spree. The hero has glutted Scamander's waters with blood and its bed with bodies. The river is so enraged that it tries to drown the hero. When Achilles finally gets to Hector, he slaughters him before the eyes of his parents, Hecuba and Priam, and drags his body across the plains of Troy. Achilles is drunk on rage, the poem tells us. His rational mind has left him, and he is mad with the joy of slaughter. The ability to modulate character that Hector shows—the fierce warrior becoming the loving father—is something Achilles does not possess. He is as mad now as a wild beast. Achilles, one feels, could not stop himself if he wished to: A fellow Greek who somehow insulted him when he was on his rampage would be in nearly as much danger as a Trojan enemy. Plato would recognize Achilles as a man who has lost all reason and who has allowed *thymos* to dominate his soul.

This ability to go mad—to become berserk—is inseparable from Achilles' greatness as a warrior. It is part of what sets him above the more circumspect Hector on the battlefield. When Hector encounters Achilles for the last time, Hector feels fear. Achilles in his wrath has no idea what fear is, and that is part of what makes him unstoppable.

Achilles' fate is too often the fate of warriors and, in a lower key, of athletes. They unleash power in themselves that they cannot discipline. They leave the field of combat or the field of play and they are still ferocious, or they can be stirred to ferocity by almost nothing. They can let no insult pass. A misplaced word sends them into a rage. A mild frustration turns them violent. *Thymos*, as Plato would have said, has taken over their souls, and reason no longer has a primary place—in some cases it has no place at all.

The kind of intensity that sports—and especially kinetic sports like football—can provoke is extremely necessary for any society: *Thymos* must have its moment. But that intensity is mortally dangerous for society and for individuals, too. Sports can lead people to brutal behavior—I see no way to avoid the conclusion. To any dispassionate observer it is clear that athletes find themselves in more brawls, more car wrecks, more spousal assaults, more drunken-driving episodes than the average run of the population. Sports can teach people to modulate their passions—they can help them be closer to Hector. But they can foment cruelty as well. Athletes, as everyone who went to an American high school will tell you, can be courtly, dignified individuals. But they're often bullies as well; they often seek violence for its own sake. They take crude pleasure in dominating others; they like to humiliate their foes off the field as well as on.

All too often, the players who go all out on the field and can't readily turn it off when they're outside their games are the best players. They're the most headlong, the most fearless, the most dedicated. And when they encounter a modulated, more controlled antagonist in a game, often the more brutal player wins.

The great athlete runs on instinct—everyone knows that. But a by-product of running on instinct is that you lose the habit of thought. Thought is what slows you down, makes you overly self-conscious, and gives the other guy time to beat you to the ball. Listening to most sports figures talk is like listening to the paint dry, and this is not necessarily because they don't have any mental endowments. It seems rather that to develop that kind of spontaneity that sports require, you have to stifle the mental endowments that you do have: The habit of thought will only take you so far as an athlete or as a hand-to-hand warrior. It does happen that great athletes can show an inclination for thinking: Muhammad Ali had the inclination, but not much ability; Bill Russell seems to have had some of both. But this is not common, and for good reason.

Lawrence Taylor was one of the best players ever to play in the National Football League. With his speed and ferocity and his ability to run down the opposing quarterback, he made football into a different, more violent game. But he was often as much in a fury off the field as on. By his own account, Taylor led the life of a beast: Drunk, brawling, high on coke, speeding in his car, he was a peril to anyone who came near him. His coach, Bill Parcells, helped him to cultivate this off-field character, knowing that it contributed to his prowess when he played. If the best players are—or often are—the ones who are the least controlled, the ones in whom at all times passion for preeminence trumps reason, then it is not entirely clear that one can readily say what American coaches and boosters of all sorts love to say, that sports always build character. If having a good character means having a coherent, flexible internal structure where the best part rules over the most dangerous, then sports may not always be something conducive to true virtue.

My own experience in high school confirms this view. Playing football made me more confident; it gave me powers of resolve that I'd draw on later in life, and I'm grateful for those things. But it also made me more brutal. I came to crave the physical stimulation of the game—I came to like hitting and even being hit. When the season ended, I found myself recreating the feeling of football in a string of fistfights and mass brawls. I didn't become a thug—far from it. But I did let the part of me that sought power and standing—over others—go way too far. Having been down that road, the chances of my taking it again are greater, I suspect, than they are for other men. Once the path has been cut, it stays open. I once shocked a colleague, and myself, by admitting that if someone ran a light and smashed up my car (which I loved more than I should), the chances of my popping him in the jaw were probably much greater than the chances of the average professional guy doing so. Once the punch in the mouth is part of your repertoire— once you've done it a few times as an adult—it never really goes away.

There's another major difficulty with sports, especially with sports played by males. When males get together in groups, they often act badly. They appoint by quiet consensus an alpha male and they follow his lead; they become more literal, more obvious; they jostle and compete. And they're also disposed to scapegoating. Homosexuality—or any indication of homosexuality—has tended to send heterosexual male athletes into a horrible spin when they're together in groups. The male sports world has been a dramatically antigay world. Those players who are homosexual have known that they must hide it on pain of humiliation or even physical harm.

In the world of sports, hostility to homosexuals and to anything perceived as unmanly has been heightened to an extreme degree. The player enters a world of brutal distinctions—of rejection and scapegoating—and, not surprisingly, he risks becoming more brutal himself.

Sports are also—it almost goes without saying—an intensely hierarchical world. In sports your identity and prowess are one and the same. When one teammate looks at another, what he sees first is how good the other is. He makes a quick calculation: Am I more or less able than he is? Or are we, perhaps, the same? Sports are about standings, and not just of the team against other teams but within the team itself. Everyone has a place in the hierarchy, and that hierarchy is constantly shifting. This sense of relative human importance is almost completely unsentimental—there's an accuracy of evaluation in sports that presides nowhere else in the world; there's no affirmative action on a football field. Everyone on a team knows who he is better than and who is better than he, and he acts his part. On NBA teams, the alpha dog, the best player on the team, determines what tunes they'll listen to in the locker room and sets the tone for how the players will connect with the coach and how they'll comport themselves on the court with the referees and off it with the public. A world that is so intensely hierarchical is a clear, energizing world where meaning is available all the time. Who are you? I'm the best center in the league, or the second best, or whatever. And I'm working to rise, or to stay on top—or whatever. One of the joys of sports lies in knowing who you are and where you are and what you have to do to ascend. Such knowledge is not available to most people in the world and they often envy it, or they tap into it vicariously by becoming fans.

Yet a world of omnipresent hierarchy is also, by definition, a world that is low on compassion and kindness. The great spiritual teachers—Jesus, Confucius, the Buddha—taught, perhaps above every other tenet, that we are all the same and that we are all part of one great life. They taught compassion, which is the feeling that you and I and all of us live in a world of suffering and grief and that our first duty is to treat each other with loving-kindness. The world of sport is a pagan world—the agonistic world that came before the great spiritual teachers—in which compassion is not a prominent value. True, professional athletes often take part in the culture of compassion: They show up at children's hospitals and attend worthy fund-raisers. These gestures serve to salve the conscience of a public that cannot rest fully content with a world of unsentimental strife. The public has an allegiance both to such strife and to the tenets of kindness and compassion. Many Americans attend church on Sunday and listen to the loving Gospel of the Savior and then repair home to their television sets, turn on the game, and watch young men try to bust each other's spleens. We must create a variety of fictions to live comfortably with this state of affairs.

From the perspective of the great teachers, it's demeaning and foolish to reduce people to their prowess at one thing or another. When I was at my best playing football, I was counted as one of the pack, a genuine player, and it put some bounce in my step. Now a late-career pickup basketball player, I'm the guy who misses too many jump shots in a row and gets the ball taken away from him by quicker guys—and while I'm on the court, that's all I am. The rest of my identity is eclipsed by it. The great teachers tell us that the only road to happiness is having a sense of common being with all others we see and acting out of that sense at all times. When you do so, you lose your meager and vain individuality in something larger and you can stop striving, stop desiring to ascend. You can rest. The more ambitious you are, the more competitive you are, the less often the feeling of serene being—in which, as Wordsworth says, "with an eye made quiet by the power of harmony and the deep power of joy, we see into the life of things"—will come your way. The individual who lives in such a spirit, Schopenhauer tells us, is the one who, when he passes another on the street, says to himself, "That too is me." Those who whisper, however subliminally, "That is another," live in the purgatory of individual pride and individual desire. Do sports encourage you to be part of a group, the team? The team, to this way of thinking, is simply an extension of "me," since it is defined by the desire for supremacy over others.

Do sports build character? Sports are what Derrida, in an essay on Plato, associates with something called the *pharmakon*, a substance that is both a poison and a remedy. Sports can do great good: build the body, create a stronger, more resilient will, impart confidence, stimulate bravery, and even foment daring. But at the same time, sports can and often do brutalize the player—they make him more violent, more aggressive. They make him intolerant of gentleness; they help turn him into a member of the pack, which defines itself by maltreating others: the weak, the differently made. One might say that the use of intelligence is needful here. One must think hard and think well and, in Plato's spirit, one must use the mind to give the thymotic drives of the soul full recognition and reasonable play, but at the same time to keep them in check. This is an ideal— Hector's ideal, we might call it—and it is not an impossible one. But there is something in the drive for glory that despises all reflection. A certain sort of glory seeking must in fact overcome reflection, as Achilles shows. So sports will always be a world of danger, as well as one rich with human possibility.

GLORIOUS FAILURE
2005 Convocation Address,
University of Virginia

THANK YOU. I'M very pleased and very honored to be
here, and without false modesty, I really feel a certain
amount of doubt that I have anything new to say to so distinguished and successful a group of people, but thank you anyway
for asking me.

I'm addressing, I know, some of the most accomplished students at the university and also their parents, people who've had
great success in one of the most difficult of all arts, the art of
raising children. I myself have children and I think I can begin to understand what this day means to the parents and the
grandparents and sisters and brothers and uncles who've made
the trip to Charlottesville, and from my heart, warmest congratulations for what you've achieved and what is likely to be
achieved in the future.

This is, as I say, a remarkably successful group of people, and
what I'm going to be talking about is not success at all. What
I'm going to be talking about is failure and the necessary role
that failure plays in anything that would qualify as authentic

success. I'm going to come out in favor of failure. I'm going to say some good things in behalf of it. I'm going to enjoin you before you leave this university, and maybe sometime afterward, to fail a little bit more.

But before I do that, I want to tell you something. Let me put it this way—it's a narrative, and if you laugh, it's a joke; if you nod your head wisely, it's a story; and if you get up and leave, it's really bad. Here it is. Once upon a time there was a man named Joseph. He was a good husband, a good father, a good provider. He lived well in the world. He was also a religious man. He prayed regularly, gave money to his church; he was upright, good, and strong. He had everything he wanted in the world except for one thing. He wanted more than anything else to win the lottery, so he would pray regularly and he would say, "Oh, Lord, I've been a good man. I've sacrificed, I've prayed. I've held up my end of the bargain. Please, I would like to win the lottery." Years went by. Still no lottery win. Joseph became a little more insistent—"Lord, I've sacrificed, I've prayed, I've done your good works, I've done your bidding in every way. Now, what about that lottery?"

This goes on for years until Joseph begins to get a little bit irritated with the Lord. "Lord, when am I going to win the lottery?" Still nothing. Finally, one day Joseph begins to entreat the Lord again and a voice comes to him as from above. It says, "Joseph."

"Hmmm, yes."

"This is the Lord."

"Finally. Lord, I've sacrificed, I've prayed, I've been an upright and good man. I've done all of your bidding. When am I going to win the lottery?"

"Joseph, be calm."

"Lord, please, when?"

"Joseph, I have one piece of advice for you."

"Lord, what is it? I'll do anything."

"Joseph, buy a ticket."

Buy a ticket. That's the subject of my talk. Well, you laughed, so it turned out to be a joke. I'm very glad about that.

The last time I was here in U Hall, I have to admit the joke was on me. I took my son, whom I'm very proud to have here today, to a concert by a guy named Ludacris, who's a rapper. I like Ludacris a lot. It turned out that none of the other parents were available to take their children to that show. I don't really know why. And I sat up in section 32, right there, and I was enjoying the show, and then suddenly the person who was standing roughly where I am now—that was Ludacris—looked up and said something like this: "I want to send one out to the elderly dude jamming in the back."

And it was strange because I was up there by myself and I looked around for the elderly dude and I didn't see him and then 'Cris—I call him 'Cris because we're kind of friendly—helped me out by having somebody shine a big spotlight up there, so I could look for the elderly dude. But the problem was the light was really in my eyes and I couldn't see him for anything.

You know Oscar Wilde's great line? The tragedy of getting older is not that one is old, it's that one is young. I know what you thought I was going to say—I like Ludacris. I know you thought I was going to say something bad about your music, rap and all that. I know you did. But you know, from a baby boomer perspective, the way we sometimes look at it is this: You gave us Britney Spears and we gave you the Rolling Stones. It's hardly fair.

Well, that was a bittersweet moment that Ludacris provided for me here. I'm pleased to revisit the scene of that semitrauma and fundamentally to have it healed by President Casteen's very generous introduction of me.

But as he was talking about the list of my accomplishments—of which I'm duly proud, I suppose—I flashed on something else that I often have occasion to think about. Those are things that come off my résumé and, as I say, it's a good and fine résumé and many of you who are out there today are compiling résumés that will be better and finer by far. But one of the things I think about when I hear that résumé is another résumé that I have, and that résumé I call my ghost résumé . And what's on my ghost résumé are all the things that went awry, the essays that didn't work, the book projects that fell apart, the writing that seemed like it was coming from the pen of Samuel Johnson on Tuesday and turned out on Friday not to make much sense at all.

I think about my first book, *Towards Reading Freud*, Princeton University Press. The struggle to get that book published, the war to get that book published, is something that I dare say Napoleon would've admired. It was a two-year push, maybe three. But it doesn't say that on the résumé. It simply says, "Princeton University Press." It just says all of the good stuff. There's a whole litany of failures there back behind the accomplishments, and they continue to happen. I continue to try things that don't work, try things that half work, try things that need to be revised five times before they're ever going to work.

When I was a young man I had a myth of my own. It's the myth of arrival, and what that myth said was that at a certain point you get to a place in your career and everything goes well. Everything you do works, because you're a success and that's that. I'm here to tell you that that point does not exist. But I'm proud of those failures because they made possible what successes I was able to achieve. I surprised myself occasionally, and that felt pretty good. Yeats said, "That which fascinates is the most difficult among things not impossible." And I've always wanted to be fascinated by what I'm doing, and that means I've done difficult things. Or at least things that have been difficult for me. If you do difficult things, take on truly challenging ventures, you will at least occasionally fail. But you'll be fascinated, too. You'll be awake.

I was a student of failure for a long time. I've watched people who are remarkable successes, the people I admired most, going through their lives compiling failure after failure. The first person I encountered in that regard and the one whose work really changed my life was Malcolm X. I remember reading Malcolm X's book. It was the first book that I ever bought with my own money, a book that I read all the way through without stopping, as I recall it. It just fascinated me. I remember Malcolm X as a street thug going to jail in Boston. He lived close to me. I remember him going to jail and getting into arguments in the prison yard and feeling that he couldn't keep up with the arguers. Though he was smart, he had a good mind, he didn't know much. And he knew that the way to learn something was to read, and he went to the prison library and he got out as many books as he could. He said: I went down those pages and fifteen, twenty words were words I didn't know. So I went and I got the dictionary and I started reading the dictionary but I didn't remember the words, so I copied down the words and I copied down their definitions. I copied the whole dictionary. You can't believe what a world opened up to me at that point, Malcolm X said.

He had led a miserable failure of a life, and suddenly he was an intellectual and a dynamic man. He went on from there to be a preacher among the black Muslims for the Reverend Elijah Muhammad—dramatic, not always right in my view, but surely provocative all the time. He provoked thought—that's what Malcolm did. Everywhere he went, he provoked thinking. He went on to embrace a different kind of Islam in which he held out hope for the brotherhood of all regardless of color. Malcolm X was somebody who looked back repeatedly, looked back on failures as well as successes, and used those failures as an opportunity to do something else. He didn't have one life or two. He had three or four because of the resiliency that he possessed.

Another one of my heroes in the art of failure is Walt Whitman. Walt Whitman at the age of thirty-two was absolutely nothing, absolutely nothing. He was not good at anything. He taught school for a while and he was bad at that and for this reason: He refused to whip his students. He wrote temperance novels of an unreadable badness. He wrote newspaper pieces that really don't hold up anymore. But then suddenly reading Emerson and going to the opera and walking the streets of New York City and writing in his notebook, strange and wonderful thoughts started to come to pass. Suddenly Whitman was writing ecstatically—outside himself—and the result of that amazing faith in his own possibilities amidst failure was the best book of American poetry, from my point of view, ever written, *Leaves of Grass*. He sent it off to the most formidable literary figure in America at the time, Ralph Waldo Emerson, Emerson, somebody who combined all the prestige of every American Nobel Prize winner alive today. Emerson took the volume, read it, and said, "I find it the finest piece of wit and wisdom that America has yet contributed." And he told Whitman as much, and Whitman printed it on the spine of the book and sent it out. Good for him.

Whitman went on to live the life that he imagined in *Song of Myself* and in *Leaves of Grass*. In the 1860s, he became a male nurse in the hospitals in Washington. He tended the men, the wounded, Union troops and Confederate both. He took their letters down. He gave them small presents. He made their last moments at least something like bearable. He'd walk in the street in the morning and exchange glances with Abraham Lincoln and I like to think that the two of them recognized each other as having something quite unusual, because if you're going to look for failure in American literature and American history: How many elections did Abraham Lincoln win? Not many. Not many, but he came back every time.

Failure is a big part of education, it seems to me, and we're lucky at the University of Virginia because our most exemplary figures are figures who were not successful all the time, not even close to it. I'm pleased and proud to be wearing my doctoral robes from Yale University, but Yale was a school where I often felt you had it or you didn't, you knew it or you didn't, whereas at Virginia I feel there are many, many chances.

The life of Edgar Allan Poe, Virginia's most famous graduate, was a disaster, right? Alcohol problems, health problems, gambling problems, every deficiency under the sun. For a while, one of the great scholarly debates in Poe studies was whether in fact he had died drunk and in the gutter or not. Whether he died that way or not, it was not unhabitual for Poe to be loaded and half out of his head. Yet he turned out a spectacular amount of writing, not just the short stories but a novel, essays, and critical studies. He was a reviewer like nobody else. He worked ferociously and he opened up a whole nightmare world in his art, the world of the House of Usher, the world of all those horrible tales. Introduced us to nightmares; in some ways he pioneered the art of psychoanalysis and developed gothic art, which has its resonances in some of the best writing going on today—as well as in *Saw II* through *XXXX*.

I think of Thomas Jefferson, a true cultural and political hero, author of the Declaration of Independence, Statutes of Religious Freedom, founder of the University of Virginia, and yet in many ways a deeply flawed man in his relations to his slaves. The way he treated Sally Hemings and the children he bore with her doesn't bear easy consideration. But I like to think of Jefferson as somebody who on some level, acknowledging his flaws, helped in his way to make people in posterity free in ways that he himself couldn't make the people around him free. When the revelations finally came out about Jefferson and Sally Hemings, the response that I heard from a number of black people, charitable in their response to failure, went like this— it's good finally to be able to welcome Thomas Jefferson into the family.

One problem with success is that people ask you to do the successful things over and over and over again. We all know people who've written the same book, painted the same picture, sung the same song time and time and time again. There's a wonderful moment on a Joni Mitchell album when she says, after somebody asked her to do "Circle Game" one more time, "You know, nobody ever said to Van Gogh, 'Paint *A Starry Night* again, man.'" But the wonderful thing about Joni Mitchell is that she has tried everything in music. She's worked with jazz musicians, she's done folk rock, she's composed on her own. Her originality is simply stunning. Her breadth is stunning. Most of us now know her as the voice of the sixties. She's more than that. She's a good painter, too. One time I saw Joni Mitchell, it was in New York City and she had a big band with her. That was the experiment of the day. It was simply awful, but I was pleased to pay my enormous sum. I felt like I'd given each member of the band about five dollars in order to continue a career of tremendous failure and tremendous success.

Is it F. Scott Fitzgerald who said there are no second acts in American life? It's possible that in an American life there's nothing but second acts. Hillary Rodham Clinton was in many ways in disgrace for eight years; the remark about cookies was just the beginning of it; the failure of the health care plan with Ira Magaziner; thoughtless remarks; the embarrassment of living with Bill. As they say in Arkansas, he's a dog who won't always stay on the porch. But now she's reinvented herself and become one of the most respected, tough-minded, intelligent, and hardworking—however you think about her politics—people in the United States Senate. A second act in American life. And there surely must be second acts in American life when you can turn on the TV and see Donald Trump standing there in front of you.

One way to think about education and what we're trying to do here is that we want to give a dramatic second chance to people. People come to us having been lovingly socialized by their mothers and fathers, by their ministers and priests, and by their families, and as beautiful as that process of socialization is, sometimes it fails, sometimes it doesn't work. People need to find a new way to talk about themselves and their worlds. People need to find a new thing to be. People need, as it were, a rebirth, often of a secular sort. In my classes, they sometimes learn from Wordsworth how much nature truly means to them and how much guarding the natural world can do. They learn from Blake what it means to be an energized prophet for social change, or they learn from Jane Austen what it can mean to be somebody who loves the world as it is and lives happily within it.

This need for a second chance, this need for change, is no insult to the parents who've socialized our students the first time through. Parental love is like the sun—it's bright and endless and free and is often never thanked, but provides people with the confidence to take another chance, to do another thing, to start again.

I've talked about a lot of people here in my pantheon— Hillary Clinton and Donald Trump and, more seriously, Thomas Jefferson and Edgar Allan Poe, but I want to end with one particular hero of mine, Saul Bellow, who died this year. Bellow was a simply amazing writer with a huge achievement, but what was the best moment of his life, he tells us, came in the midst of failure. He was in Paris in his thirties on a Guggenheim Fellowship. He had just finished publishing two novels, a little bit sterile, a little bit staid. "I wrote them," he said, "to satisfy the English professors," at which my heart quails a little bit. He was halfway through another novel about two brothers living in a mental institution, as I remember—dismal stuff. "At a certain point," he said, "in the middle of Paris not hearing English anymore, away from my own everyday language, the language became precious and rare and more intimate and immediate to me and I began to write something entirely new, something that was entirely a surprise to myself."

That surprise became a book called *The Adventures of Augie March*, and in it Bellow is successful in creating a new voice. I'll read you a couple of lines from it and you'll see. Here's the beginning: "I am an American," says Augie, "Chicago born—

Chicago, that somber city—and go at things as I have taught myself, free-style, and will make the record in my own way: first to knock, first admitted; sometimes an innocent knock, sometimes a not so innocent." It's beautiful stuff. Then, fifteen hundred manuscript pages later, Bellow, looking back through Augie's eyes, trying to figure out if he's made anything at all or if he's failed again and maybe half-satisfied if he has, says, "I may well be a flop in this line of endeavor. Columbus too thought he was a flop, probably, when they sent him back in chains. Which didn't prove there was no America."

Let me close by asking you to succeed as much as you can, but in the process of succeeding, I hope that you'll generate a really remarkable ghost résumé made of the failures that come from trying to do things that you need to do, that are hard to do, and that are demanding to do. Whether it seems in character or not, it's often the time to start the band, to write the poem, to begin the business, to initiate anything that's new and challenging and difficult.

I told you that story which turned out to be a joke about buying a ticket. But there's one thing I didn't tell you. Tickets are expensive. It's hard to draft that novel, hard to get the band together, hard to learn how to shoot a movie. Tickets are expensive, especially the risky ones, but they're infinitely worth buying. So buy a ticket, buy a ticket, buy one.

Thanks.

THE GLOBALISTS

MEMBERS OF THE Chinese Red Army are boarding our ship. I'm a hundred yards from the gangway, but still I recognize them. They're wearing dome-shaped hats with snap earmuffs. The red stars pinned to the center of the khaki domes, like the Buddhist third eye, the eye of wisdom, are sparkling. We—seven hundred students and forty or so faculty members sailing with an outfit called Semester at Sea—docked here in Shanghai, China, yesterday. The city is polluted as a cesspool and it's booming. We're told that on a good day you can't see the sun until two o'clock in the afternoon and that it's gone by three o'clock, four tops. Today there's been no sun, period, only smoke and fog so dense that you feel like you could reach out and grab a handful and roll it up like a dirty snowball. It's surprising I can see those stars twinkling Maoist red on the heads of the cadres, but I can.

Hold on, though. Those aren't Red Army troops: They're our students. Obviously they've picked up the hats in the souvenir kiosks in town. Some are wearing T-shirts featuring Chairman Mao; others are wearing straw harvest-the-rice domes, also bedecked with red stars. Have the kids gone communist? Are they turning pink?

What they're supposed to be doing is getting a global education. They're supposed to be in the process of becoming citizens of the world. That's the objective of our trip, which has taken us to Brazil and South Africa, Mauritius and Malaysia and India, and will hit Vietnam and Japan before we're done. We're off to acquire a "global education." That seems to be the hot term now in higher-ed circles. But when I ask around among my colleagues—well-traveled, dedicated types—they don't seem to have much more idea what global education is than I do. (And I haven't got any idea at all.) I've taken to watching the students to see if they might offer a hint. It'll have to be a visual cue, I'm afraid: Like my colleagues, they don't seem disposed to ready definitions. They're on the ship, most of them say, to see the world and to have a good time.

Pretty quickly I learn that the Red Army togs don't have anything to do with a new Marxist consciousness and commitment to the Little Red Book. The students think the hats and T-shirts look cool, period. They like the screaming red of the stars; they like the dour, doughy face of the chairman as much as Andy Warhol did—and they're too young to have heard Lennon tell them what doesn't happen to people who go around carrying his image.

But what do the Chinese on the streets of Shanghai think when they see Americans decked out in Marxwear? Probably something like what we would think if we saw Chinese tourists marching down Fifth Avenue wagging American flags. We'd figure they were crazy about the U.S.A. We'd think we were the shining apple of their eye. Presumably the Chinese who see the regalia think that our kids are in love with China. They must feel that the American visitors somehow support—or at least accept—the regime, with its commitment to one-party rule: no freedom of speech, no press freedom, limited freedom of religion, no significant freedom to assemble. The preeminent freedom in China now is the freedom to make money.

Our young globalists needed to think twice about their wardrobes. When classes started again on the ship, there were more than a few sessions about political life in current China and what it meant to appear to endorse it. It was time to talk about the price of political naïveté, and many of us teachers did.

But our students—our budding globalists—brought something besides their naïveté to China and to the other countries we visited. They brought something that, from what I can tell, America excels in exporting. They brought friendliness. Everywhere we went we saw the kids on the street, palling around with local people, trying to speak their language, making jokes, hacking around. They'd talk to anyone they met—rich or poor, old or young. If the people they met knew English, well and good. If not, our kids went to sign language or strained to pick up a few words of the local tongue. The students told their life stories and heard their new pals' tales in exchange. One of my students said he spent three hours talking with the eighty-year-old owner of a dinky restaurant he ate at in Shanghai. "I never laugh so much," she said to him at the end of the evening. "You my crazy American son." Another student told me about meeting everyone on hand in a bar in Malaysia. "We loved them," he said. "And I think they were jazzed we were there."

To my eye, the people the kids encountered in China and Vietnam and India and Brazil and all the other places we went *were* jazzed. Our gang stormed onto the scene, and whatever was fixed and set in the local social configuration quickly became unglued. The students stumbled around in other languages; they ate anything they were served; they almost never slept. And they were persistently, almost insanely open.

Did they get taken? Constantly. At our pre-port meeting before Shanghai, we learned about how young Chinese students would come on in a friendly way and then take foreign visitors off to a "traditional" tea ceremony. Two hours later, their friendly hosts would hit them with bills for seventy-five dollars for a couple of cups of tea and a few grains of rice. Did our students heed the warnings? Of course they didn't. "I felt bad getting ripped off like that," one of them, who didn't have money to spare, told me, "but to tell you the truth, I really liked the girls who did it, and they taught me a lot about China. Anyway. I had fun." People who are morbidly afraid of being taken are among the worst kinds of travelers—suspicious and locked down like clams. They'll get into a half-hour verbal brawl with a taxi driver over two dollars. They'll be so steamed about it all day that they can't enjoy the bronzes in the Shanghai Museum or the street life in Hong Kong. Our kids were never afraid of being taken. When they got mad—everyone who travels gets mad—they were over it in five minutes.

"Sometimes," one of my colleagues said, "our students think that they can replace politeness with friendliness." Well, they did seem to feel that way—if you didn't move fast on that ship, they could run you down. And it was not always a good idea to get between them and the dessert trays, especially when the ship was pitching. Politeness wasn't their long suit.

But having seen them in action on shore and listened to their stories, I'm persuaded that friendliness does trump politeness, and with ease. American friendliness was surely behind a pronouncement we heard a thousand times: "We're not so happy with American government, but Americans? We like them a lot." The kids provided commercial opportunity to almost all who encountered them (they generally seemed to have more money than was good for them; more money, say, than their worthy professors), but that wasn't the whole story. Living in America, it's easy to forget how stratified many cultures are. The caste system isn't strictly legal in India anymore, but there's no doubt that it's still in play. (Indians I met claimed they could recognize another person's caste at a glance.) In South Africa, even after apartheid, the old racial categories still abide. The first conversation I had there was with a cab driver, a Xhosa, who told a nasty joke about the foreskin of the Zulu running for president. Among the Chinese, your education level seems to determine who you are and how you are treated.

This isn't to say that America's a country without class distinctions. But America is a country where nearly the worst thing you can be is a snob. A rich guy isn't worth much, by our account, if he can't yak a little about baseball or the movies with the guy who mows his lawn or the woman who bags the groceries. (Granted, this is in part because the rich guy may be bagging groceries or mowing lawns a year from now.) The unpardonable American social crime is looking down your nose at someone. The great public virtue is being open and easygoing—the great public virtue is friendliness. Our students brought friendliness abroad in barrels, our equivalent of export oil.

The laureate of this sort of thing is Walt Whitman, who began his own anonymous review of his first volume with the words, "An American bard at last!" Almost every American who looks into Whitman understands his egalitarian side immediately. It's rare, at least in my experience, that non-Americans do. (D.H. Lawrence, for example, seemed to think that Whitman

was out of his mind.) "Walt Whitman, an American," the hobo
bard chants in "Song of Myself":

> *one of the roughs, a kosmos,*
> *Disorderly fleshy and sensual . . . . eating and drinking and*
>   *breeding,*
> *No sentimentalist . . . . no stander above men and women or apart*
>   *from them . . . . no more modest than immodest.*

"No stander above men and women or apart from them":
That's the key phrase. "By God!" he says later in the same section, "I will accept nothing that all cannot have their counter-
part of on the same terms." My students read these passages—with
the waves slapping away on the side of the classroom—and by
and large they bought them. Maybe on some level they already
knew what Whitman had to tell them.

But, you may say, the reason that the kids are so open and
appealing is that they're innocents. Their naïveté is what's be-
guiling. And part of what creates that innocence is ignorance.
They don't go from place to place pressed to the ground with
the burden of the past—in part because they don't know much
about that past. They go around grinning, wearing Red Army
regalia, with no real clue about the horrors of the Cultural
Revolution.

Maybe there's some truth in this indictment. But if so, it
makes clear what one objective of a genuine college education
now might be—for students and teachers both. Do the students
need historical instruction? Sure, so do we all. If we're going to
be global citizens, we'd better know something about the biog-
raphy of the globe. But I wonder if it would be possible for our
students to learn as much and still keep alive the quality that

really does make them stand out in the best possible way. They broke a lot of ice on our trip, even if they did drive me half crazy with the stuff they didn't know and didn't always want to know. And truly, I couldn't say I was half as open as they were. I didn't meet as many people, didn't show all of those I did meet what was best about America. Is it possible to combine knowledge and friendliness? Could we educate our students (and ourselves) in the ways of both global innocence and global experience? If we could, maybe we'd be creating citizens of the world, American style.

THE CORPORATE CITY AND
THE SCHOLARLY ENCLAVE

WHERE SHOULD YOU go to college—assuming you're a high school student and getting ready for this new phase of your life? Where should you encourage your son or daughter to go—assuming that you're a parent?

As a college professor, I get asked the where-to-go question frequently, and I know that all of us teaching in colleges and universities do too. How should one answer? What is the right thing to say to someone deciding on his or her future? For myself, I'm inclined to respond by posing another question.

Are you looking for a corporate city, or are you looking for a scholarly enclave?

Neither of these kinds of schools exists in its pure form. To the scholarly enclave, even the most ideal, there will always be a practical, businessy dimension. Somebody's got to keep the books and pay the bills. And even in the most corporate of colleges, there will be islands of relative scholarly idealism.

Many, if not most, American high school students have already had a taste of the corporate city. These are students and parents who are emerging from the mouth of that great American dragon called the "good high school." I won't hide my prejudices: I have a lot of qualms about the good American high school. Most good high schools now look to me like credential factories. They are production centers that kids check in to every day. The motivated, success-oriented students set to work from the moment of arrival, producing something, manufacturing something. And what they produce are credentials. High schools now are credential factories in overdrive.

It doesn't mean that students don't have to work to get those credentials: Of course they do. It takes lots of effort, planning, and organization—and it takes some smarts—to get what students, the workers in the high school factory, are out to get. Students feel that they need to get A's—they need to excel in their courses. They also feel they need to stimulate the goodwill of their teachers and their guidance counselors: Those recommendations are crucial. Students in high school now also need to rack up lots of extracurriculars: They need to do some community service; they need to be president (or, maybe better, treasurer) of a club or two; it's good as well if they can play at least one varsity sport, or, if they are prone to stumbling over their own feet (as I was in high school), they can at least manage a team or keep the uniforms clean.

High school now is about being an all-arounder. You've got to be good at your classes, but you've also got to shine as a citizen and a general hand-waving, high-enthusiasm participant. To do this, you've often got to make yourself into a superb time manager. You give each activity the amount of time and effort required so that you can reach the so-called standard of excellence. You give it that much, but you give it no more. Do I really need to read the whole book to get an A in English, the student asks herself? Probably she doesn't. Do I need a tutor and extra time to score a top grade in math? Perhaps yes. If so, the money is well spent and so is the time. Will it look better to put in two hours a week volunteering at the hospital or four at the soup kitchen? Does the guidance counselor say that both will look about the same to the college admissions board? Then better to do the hospital: You'll need those extra two hours for prom committee.

High school students need to produce A's. High school students need to produce credentials. No A's, no first-tier college (probably). No credentials, no grandly embossed letters of acceptance—or at least no chirpy e-mail notifications of entrance into the class of 2017.

You'll discern here that I'm not entirely approving of the good American high school and its MO—but on some level I think that I understand what's up. Even if the current mode of high school education—for the good student at the good high school—doesn't especially appeal to a student, what is she supposed to do about it? A fifteen-year-old standing up at a school meeting and saying that she's mad as heck about being slapped on an assembly line, or that she's mad at her parents for slapping here there, or that she's mad at herself—that's not going to do very much. She's going to feel alone and lonely and sad, and anyway she may not even be able to find the words to express her feelings. She probably hasn't read about or even heard the name Mario Savio, who made a speech at the University of California, Berkeley, in 1964. I understand that quite often high school history courses now don't take you all the way up through the period of the Vietnam War, but stop at the end of World War II because "we've run out of time."

Mario Savio stood up at Sproul Plaza at Berkeley and said that as a college student, as a Berkeley student, he too often felt like a piece of raw material that was getting processed by his university and by his society. He believed that many of his contemporaries felt the same way. And then he talked back to that condition. He said, "But we're a bunch of raw materials that don't mean to be—have any process upon us. Don't mean to be made into any product! Don't mean—Don't mean to end up being bought by some clients of the university, be they the government, be they industry, be they organized labor, be they anyone! We're human beings!" We're not products, Mario Savio says: We're human beings. He says it in a broken-up Bob Dylan and Woody Guthrie sort of way, but he says it. Probably a young guy or girl going to high school now hasn't heard of Mario Savio or listened to his famous lines from Sproul Plaza.

They are lines to which young people will respond differently. Some may say: I love high school. I love the hustle and bustle and the classes and the clubs and the staying up late and the social life and the prom and the messing with Facebook. I love striving for success. I like the game and I like the rewards of the game, and so—give me some more.

Some rising high school seniors may be ready for more of the same—assuming what I've said about American high schools now is right or half right. And if so, they need to apply to and eventually install themselves in the kind of college I call the corporate city.

What do you get there in the corporate city? You get more of the same. Everyone is on the make; everyone is trying to succeed. A tremendous amount of networking goes on because people have come to realize that as the old saying runs, It's often not what you know but who you know. Students still study. But in the old high school tradition, you study only as much as you need to study to get your A's. If expedient but slightly shady means of A-getting arise, you may even evaluate them using a risk-reward equation. That is, you balance what can be gained against the pains of getting caught. And even if you don't cheat per se, you're always ready to cut academic corners. Do I really have to read all of *King Lear* to ace the test? Probably you don't. At a certain point—tragic inevitability being what it is—you probably know what's going to happen to the king and to Cordelia, too. When in doubt, turn to the Spark Notes or the cyber equivalent thereof.

You'll have to get by on only a little sleep—but there are ways to make that possible, some quite legal, the others semi-legal (legal, that is, for the person for whom the Adderall prescription was originally written, but perhaps not legal for you). You'll be awake and alert for as much as twenty hours of the twenty-four doing a hypercharged version of what you did in high school. You'll be meeting people, connecting with future allies for the wars of life, succeeding in your courses, engaging in lots of activities. In short, you'll be doing more than building your résumé. You'll be putting your résumé on steroids.

Universities that have made themselves into corporate cities are not hard to spot. Most of the students—and many members of the faculty—are buzzing from place to place, always feeling a bit self-important, always feeling a bit behind, like that poor rabbit in *Alice in Wonderland*. The people who represent corporate universities to you—the tour guides and the rest—will talk a lot about new computer initiatives, about partnering with business, and about the creation of young leaders. They'll talk about recent grads who have hit the Silicon Valley jackpot. These are near kids who have made pots of money and—one feels this by implication—are soon going to spread some around their former school, to which they are extremely grateful. You'll hear the word *excellence* about a billion times.

Now, even in the middle of corporate universities, you will find people who are not playing the game. These are not necessarily people who don't show up at a boring class, who smoke a lot of weed, who read books that aren't assigned, who play in bands with bizarre names, and who wear T-shirts that are distressingly original. Though sometimes they are. But what truly characterizes people who are living in, or who want to live in, a scholarly enclave?

It's pretty simple, really. They are at school seeking knowledge so as to make the lives of other human beings better. They will not tell you this when you ask them about it in casual conversation. But it is true. They want to be teachers and scientists and soldiers and doctors and legal advocates for the poor. They want to contribute something to curing cancer; they want to make sure the classics of Roman literature don't die; they want to get people excited about the art of Picasso and maybe inspire people to make some (Picasso-inspired) art of their own; they want to be sure that when a foreign nation is inclined to threaten (I mean really threaten) the peace of the United States of America, that nation has to think twice and twice again.

Do these people want some recognition? Do they want to get paid? Yes, in varying degrees they do. There are very few people who are entirely unselfish in this world, and sometimes they don't live too long. But the people I'm talking about often put others first. They have a love for humanity in them, and it is this love that chiefly motivates what they do, even if they don't tell you so every five minutes. They want to make the world better and they are honest with themselves about doing this: They know that any quest that involves status and enrich-ment is dangerous and that it can take them away from what really matters. They know that the human capacity for self-deception is boundless and they are always on the lookout for the moment when their pride eclipses their love for the world.

How do you find these people, and how do you find the schools where they are plentiful—what I've called the scholarly enclaves? That is, how do you find them if they are what you are looking for? You visit, you look, and you listen. When people start talking about leadership and incentives (and especially something called "incentivizing") and becoming an academic entrepreneur, you are probably in the wrong place. (Whenever people make fritters of English, I daresay that you're in the wrong place.) When people talk about innovation and "part-nering" with big-money institutions, I would advise you to run. If you hear the word *excellence* more than twice in a sen-tence, you are hereby empowered to pop the speaker twice (but very gently) in the nose.

Why is *excellence* a bad word? It's not, in and of itself. But people around universities who use it are people who want to talk about worldly distinction without talking about eth-ics. *Excellence* means we're smart, we're accomplished, we're successful—and we can be these things without any obligation to help our fellow human beings. When colleges start talking about "humane excellence" or "generous excellence," then I'll want to listen.

You also have my permission—in fact my encouragement—to gently snout-pop people who talk about "leadership." Why is leadership so bad? In itself, it's not. But what people usually mean by a leader now is someone who, in a very energetic, upbeat way, shares all of the values of the people who are in charge.

Leaders tend to be little adults, little grown-ups who don't challenge the big grown-ups who run the place. Grown-ups—people like me—need to be challenged, and we rely on young people to do it. When people say "leaders" now, what they mean is gung ho "followers." As an English professor, I don't really care for Mario Savio's grammar and diction. But was he an authentic leader? Was he someone who offered students a new and controversial way to think of their lives and then to live their lives? Yes, I think that he was. But no college dean or president, now or ever, would use the word *leader* to describe Mario: Most of them reserve the word for followers, for people who follow them.

The residents of scholarly enclaves are harder to spot than the denizens of the corporate university, and I can't give you a definitive field guide to finding them. But I'll say first that they don't talk about being a leader and being an entrepreneur. They talk about working in a lab or developing a questionnaire for psychological research or writing a novel, or getting people who don't belong in jail out of jail, or defending their country against its enemies. And they are not smiling all the time. They are aware of the enormous gap between what humans aspire to and what remains to be done. They tend to take joy in their work, but they never feel that they have quite gotten it right. The people in the corporate university are forever pleased with themselves. They are always succeeding, getting A's that will soon be converted into dollars.

Their view is often that everyone wants the same things that they do. They think that people who claim to work for humanity want wealth and fame too—the achievers are just more honest about the matter. The people who serve the poor themselves want to be rich: They are just too chicken to be candid about their desire and then, in the current vernacular, to go for it. And who knows, maybe this is true. This view has some important upholders: Freud and Nietzsche and (in his way) Adam Smith feed it, and they are anything but fools. But geniuses are not always right.

The people who dedicate themselves to helping humanity are not, let me say, sacrificing themselves to a life of pain and sorrow. In fact, it is only through unselfish effort on behalf of something larger than yourself that anything like happiness arises. The happiness-through-material-goods-and-success industry has to throw ads at you twenty-four hours a day to persuade you that its way of life is the best one. The happiness industry protests too much. Would it need to be as clamorous as it is about consumer bliss if there really was such a thing as consumer bliss?

Where should a young person now go to college? It depends. Does she want more of the good American high school with its hustle and bustle, its strivings for excellence, its fixation on leadership, its partnering and incentivizing and getting proactive, and succeeding, succeeding, succeeding? Or does she want something else?

THE ENGLISH MAJOR

L ATELY, WHEN THE time of year comes for college sopho-
mores to trundle off to the offices of their faculty advisers
to declare their majors, it's not hard to predict what's going to
happen. There will be more economics majors surely and more
business majors too. What there almost certainly won't be are
more English majors. The English major has been declining
drastically over the past decades. In 1970, about 8 percent of
students were English majors; by 2004 (the last date for which
figures are available), it was 4 percent. By now it may be down
to 2 or 3. It's distressing to me, and not just because I happen to
be an English prof. I think that a lot of students are making a
mistake—losing one of the greatest chances life offers. If I could,
I'd yell over the transoms of my colleagues' offices in economics and business and all the other purportedly success-ensuring
disciplines.

I'd tell the kids to drop what they were doing and get themselves over to the English department. I'd tell them to sign on
before it was too late.

An English major, you see, is much more than thirty-two or

thirty-six credits including a course in Shakespeare, a course on writing before 1800, and a three-part survey of English and American lit. That's the outer form of the endeavor. It's what's inside that matters. It's the character forming—or (dare I say?) Soul-making—dimension of the pursuit that counts. And what is that precisely? Who is the English major in his ideal form? What does the English major have and what does he want and what does he in the long run hope to become?

The English major is, first of all, a reader. She's got a book pup-tented in front of her nose many hours a day; her Kindle glows softly late into the night. But there are readers and there are *readers*. There are people who read to anesthetize themselves—they read to induce a vivid, continuous, and risk-free day-dream. They read for the same reason that people grab a glass of chardonnay—to put a light buzz on. The English major reads because as rich as the one life he has may be, one life is not enough. He reads not to see the world through the eyes of other people but effectively to *become* other people. What is it like to be John Milton, to be Jane Austen, to be Chinua Achebe? What is it like to be them at their best, at the top of their games? The English major wants the joy of seeing the world through the eyes of people who—let us admit it—are more sensitive, more articulate, shrewder, sharper, more alive than they themselves are. The experience of changing minds and hearts with Proust or James or Austen is one that is incomparably enriching. It makes you see that there is more to the world than you had ever imagined was possible. You see that life is bigger, sweeter, more tragic and intense—more alive with meaning than you had thought.

Real reading is *reincarnation*. There is no other way to put it. It is being born again into a higher form of consciousness than we ourselves possess. When we walk the streets of Manhattan with Walt Whitman or contemplate our hopes for eternity with Emily Dickinson, we are reborn into more ample and generous minds. "Life piled on life / Were all too little," says Tennyson's Ulysses, and he is right. Given the ragged magnificence of the world, who would wish to live only once? The English major lives many times through the astounding transportive magic of words and the welcoming power of his receptive imagination. The economics major? In all probability he lives but once. If the English major has the wherewithal for it, the energy and the openness of heart, he lives not once but hundreds of times. Not all books are worth being reincarnated into, to be sure— but those that are win Keats's sweet phrase: "a joy forever."

The economics major lives in facts and graphs and diagrams and projections. Fair enough. Without these things, we are told (and perhaps in part believe) there would be no civilized world. But the English major lives elsewhere. Remember the tale of that hoary patriarchal fish that David Foster Wallace made famous? The ancient swimmer swishes his slow bulk by a group of young carp suspended in the shallows. "How's the water?" the ancient asks. The carp keep their poise, like figures in a child's mobile, but say not a word. The old fish gone, one carp turns to another and speaks the signal line, "What's water?"

The English major knows that the water we humans swim in is not any material entity. Our native habitat is language, words, and the English major swims through them with the old fin's enlivening awareness. But all of us, as the carp's remark suggests, live in a different relation to language. I'll put it a little tendentiously: Some of us speak, others are spoken. "Language speaks man," Heidegger famously said. To which I want to reply, Not all men, not all women: not by a long shot. Did language speak Shakespeare? Did language speak Spenser? Not by a long shot. Milton, Chaucer, Woolf, Emerson? No, not even close.

What does it mean to be spoken by language? It means to be a vehicle for expression and not a shaper of words. It means to rely on clichés and preformulated expressions. It means to be a channeler, and what you channel is ad-speak and sports jargon and the latest in psychological babble. You sound not like a living man or a woman but like something much closer to a machine, trying to pass for human. You never know how you feel or what you want in life because the words at your disposal are someone else's words and don't represent who *you* are and what *you* want. You don't and can't know yourself. You don't and can't know the world.

The businessman rattles about excellence and leadership and partnering and productivity. The athlete clones away about the game plan and the coach and one play at a time and the inestimable blessing of having teammates who make it all possible. The politician proses about unity and opportunity and national greatness and what's in it for the middle class. When such people talk, they are not so much human beings as they are tape loops.

The essayist John Jeremiah Sullivan catches this sort of sensibility in its extreme form in an essay about reality TV shows. There, verbal channeling reaches an almost unimaginable degree of intensity: "big mouths spewing fantastic catchphrase fountains of impenetrable self-justification; spewing dark prayers calling on God to strike down those who would fuck with their money, their cash, and always knowing, always preaching. Using weird phrases that nobody uses except that everybody uses them now. Constantly talking about 'goals.' " "Fantastic catchphrase fountains of impenetrable self-justification": Yeah, that's about it.

The English major at her best isn't used by language; she uses it. She bends it and tropes it and inflects it with irony and lets hyperbole bloom like a firework flower when the time's right. She knows that language isn't there merely to represent the world as it is, was, and shall be. Language is there to *interpret* the world—language lets her say how she feels and lets others know.

The English major believes in talk and writing and knows that any worthwhile event in life requires commentary and analysis in giant proportion. She believes that the uncommented-upon life is not worth living. Then, of course, there is the commentary upon the comments. There must be, as Eliot says, a thousand visions and revisions before the taking of the toast and tea—and a few after as well to accompany the capons and the sack.

But I sometimes think that the English major's most habitual feeling about the linguistic solution in which she swims isn't practical at all. What she feels about language most of the time is wonder and gratitude. For language is a stupendous gift. It's been bequeathed to us by all of the foregoing generations. And it is the creation of great souls like Shakespeare and Chaucer to be sure. But language is also the creation of salesmen and jive talkers, jocks and mountebanks, hookers and heroic warriors. We spend our lives, knowingly or not, trying to say something impeccably. We long to put the right words in the right order. (That, Coleridge said, is all that poetry really comes down to.) And when we do, we are on the lip of adding something to the language. We've perhaps made a contribution, however small, to what the critic R.P. Blackmur called the stock of available reality. And when we do, we've lived for a moment with the immortals. Richard Poirier once called poetry the Olympics of Language—precisely so.

I love Wordsworth and Shakespeare and Donne. But I like it when a fellow pickup b-ball player points to a nervous guy skittering off to the bathroom just as the game's about to start: "He's taking a chicken pee." Yup—hit it on the head. I like it when in the incomparable "Juicy," Biggie Smalls describes coming up in life by letting us know that once "Birthdays was the worst days / Now we sip champagne when we thirs-tay." (And to advertise his new erotic ascent: "Honeys play me close like butter play toast.") Language, a great poem in and of itself, is all around us. We live in the lap of enormous wonder, but how rarely do most of us look up and smile in gratitude and pleasure? The English major does that all the time.

The English major: in love with language and in love with life—or at least hungry for as much life as he can hold. But there's something else, too. The English major immerses himself in books and revels in language for a purpose. You might even call it a high purpose, if you're disposed to such talk. (I sometimes am.) The English major wants to use what he knows about language and what he's learning from books as a way to confront the hardest of questions. He uses these things to try to figure out how to live. His life is an open-ended work in progress and it's never quite done, at least until he is. For to the English major the questions of life are never closed. There's always another book to read; there's always another perspective to add. He might think that he knows what's what as to love and marriage and the raising of children. But he's never quite sure. He takes tips from the wise and the almost wise that he confronts in books and sometimes (if he's stupendously lucky) in life. He measures them and sifts them and brings them to the court of his own experience. (There is a creative reading as well as a creative writing, Emerson said.) He's always ready to change his mind. Darwin on nature—or Wordsworth? Freud on love, or Percy Bysshe Shelley? Blake on sex, or Arthur Schopenhauer? Or perhaps none of the above. He doesn't give up his view easily, but it's nonetheless always up for debate and open for change. He's an unfinished guy, she's an unfinished woman. Which can be embarrassing and discomfiting from time to time, when he's with the knowing ones, the certain ones: those who are, often in all too many ways, finished.

Love for language, hunger for life, openness and a quest for truth or truths: Those are the qualities of my English major in the ideal form. But of course now we're talking about more than a mere academic major. We're talking about a way of life. We're talking about a way of living that places inquiry into how to live in the world—what to be, how to act, how to move through time—at its center. What we're talking about is a path to becoming a human being, or at least a better sort of human being than one was at the start. An English major? To me an English major is someone who has decided, against all kinds of pious, prudent advice and all kinds of fears and resistances, to major, quite simply, in becoming a person. Once you've passed that particular course of study—or at least made some significant progress on your way—then maybe you're ready to take up something else.

MY FIRST INTELLECTUAL

Doug Meyers came to Medford High School with big plans for teaching his philosophy course. Together with a group of self-selected seniors, he was going to ponder the eternal questions: beauty, truth, free will, fate, that sort of thing. The class would start out reading *The Story of Philosophy*, by Will Durant, then go on to Plato's dialogues, some Aristotle, Leibniz (a particular favorite of Meyers's), maybe just a little bit of Kant, then into a discussion of Bertrand Russell's effort to clear the whole thing up with an injection of clean scientific logic. Meyers had just graduated from Harvard. All of his intellectual aspirations were intact.

On the first day of class, we saw a short, slight man with olive skin—we thought he might be Mexican—wearing a skinny tie and a moth-eaten legacy suit with a paper clip fastened to the left lapel. On his feet were Ivy League gunboat shoes, lace-ups designed in homage to the *Monitor* and the *Merrimack*. He had hunched shoulders, a droopy black mustache, and Valentino-type eyes, deep brown, sensuous, and penitential. Even when he strove for some dynamism, as he did that first day, explaining his plans for the course, he still had a melancholy Castilian presence, the air of an instinctively comprehending reader of *Don Quixote.*

Having outlined the course, he turned away from us and began writing on the blackboard, in a script neater than any we would see from him again. It was a quotation from Nietzsche. He told us to get out our papers and pens and spend a couple of pages interpreting the quote "as a limbering-up exercise." I had never heard of Nietzsche. I had never read all the way through a book that was written for adults and that was not concerned exclusively with football.

The day before, I'd sat in the office of Mrs. Olmstead, the senior guidance counselor, whose perfume conjured up the sound of Mantovani's string section, sentimental, lush, and all-enfolding. We talked about Massachusetts Bay Community College, Salem State Teachers College; we discussed my working for the city of Medford—perhaps I'd start by collecting barrels, then graduate in time to a desk job (my father had some modest connections). I mentioned joining the marines. (I might have made it in time for the Cambodia invasion.) Nothing was resolved.

As I was mumbling my way out the door, Mrs. Olmstead began talking about a new teacher who was coming to the school, "someone we're especially proud to have." He was scheduled to teach philosophy. I didn't know what philosophy was, but I associated it with airy speculation, empty nothing; it seemed an agreeable enough way of wasting time.

So there I was in a well-lit top-floor room, wearing, no doubt, some sharp back-to-school ensemble, pegged pants and sporty dice-in-the-back-alley shoes, mildly aching from two or three football-inflected injuries, and pondering the Nietzsche quotation, which I could barely understand. I felt dumb as a rock, a sentiment with which I, at seventeen, had some prior experience. But by putting the quotation on the board, Meyers showed me that in at least one department his powers of comprehension were a few notches lower than mine. He had misunderstood Medford High School entirely. The appearances had taken him in. No doubt he'd strolled through the building on the day before students arrived; he'd seen desks, chalkboards, large windows that slid up and open with a cheering metallic gurgle, supply closets stocked full of paper and books, all the paraphernalia of education. He had seen those things and he'd believed that he was in a school, a place where people quested, by their lights and by fits and starts, for the truth, its elaborations and its antitheses.

But I had acquired a few facts that Meyers would not have been primed to receive at Harvard, or at prep school, or at any of the other places where he had filled his hours. Medford High School, whatever its appearances, was not a school. It was a place where you learned to do—or were punished for failing in—a variety of exercises. The content of these exercises didn't matter at all. What mattered was form—repetition and form. You filled in the blanks, conjugated, declined, diagrammed, defined, outlined, summarized, recapitulated, positioned, graphed. It did not matter what: English, geometry, biology, history, all were the same. The process treated your mind as though it was a body part capable of learning a number of protocols, simple choreographies, then repeating, repeating.

Our bodies themselves were well monitored. When the bell rang, we rose and filed into the corridor, stayed in line, spoke quietly if at all, entered the next class, were ordered to sit down, sit quietly, feet beneath the desk, all day long presided over by teachers, a significant fraction of whom were going—at greater or lesser velocities, ending sometimes with a bang, sometimes with subdued, heart-emptying sobs—out of their minds. At least two that I can remember had been mastered by a peculiar form of speech: You couldn't say they were talking to themselves, but they were not clearly addressing anyone on the outside, either. Poetry, Mill said, is not heard but overheard. This was overheard, but no way close to poetry. This was the way souls in purgatory mutter and carry on. When these teachers were overwhelmed—it wasn't hard to do: We stole Miss McDougle's rank book; we locked her once, briefly, in the supply closet—they called for a submaster, Sal Todaro, or, more feared, Dan O'Mara, Dandy Dan, to restore order. The place was a shabby Gothic cathedral consecrated to Order, and maybe it was not without its mercies. If you'd done what you should have at Medford High, the transition into a factory, into an office, into the marines would be something you'd barely notice; it would be painless, sheer grease.

Before Meyers arrived, I never rebelled against the place, at least not openly. I didn't in part because I believed that Medford High was the only game there was. The factories where my father and uncles worked were extensions of the high school; the TV shows we watched were manufactured to fit the tastes for escape that such places form; the books we were assigned to read in class, *Ivanhoe*, *Silas Marner*, *The Good Earth*, of which I ingested about fifty pages each, could, as I saw it then (I've never had the wherewithal to check back into them), have been written by the English teachers, with their bland, babbling goodness and suppressed hysterias. Small bursts of light came through in the Beethoven symphonies my father occasionally played at volume on our ancient stereo (the music sounded like it was coming in over a walkie-talkie) and the Motown tunes I heard on Boston's black radio station, WILD, but these sounds were not connected to any place or human possibility I knew about. So I checked out. I went low to the ground, despondent, suspicious, asleep in the outer self, barely conscious within.

This condition Doug Meyers changed. That now, however imperfectly, I can say what's on my mind, and that I know what kind of life I hope for, I owe not to him alone, of course, but to many. Doug Meyers pushed open the door to those others, though, other worlds, other minds. And pretty much on his own, Meyers taught me how to teach. I'm not sure if I've ever heard his sort of approach described before, but I think it's as good now as it was when I first encountered him almost thirty years ago.

For three months, Meyers did his best with Will Durant and *The Story of Philosophy*. We barely gave him an inch. Gubby Shea (Kevin Shea on his report cards and disciplinary citations) made enormous daisy chains out of the elastics he used to bind the advertising circulars he delivered in Jamaica Plain and Mattapan on Saturday mornings or sat, his body tight with concentrated energy, inking in all of the *o*'s in the textbook, a brilliant, futile parody of life at Medford High. Jeff Stanwick pried tufts of grass off the soles of his soccer cleats; Michael de Leo and John Aquino, wide receiver and quarterback for the Medford Mustangs (I blocked for them, sporadically), contemplated pass plays and the oncoming game with Newton, or Somerville, or Everett. Debbie Lauria was high school beautiful. Susan Rosenberg, the school's only hippie—she wore wire-rimmed glasses and work boots—conversed with Meyers on subjects no one else cared about. She and Joseph Jones were about the only ones with anything to say.

Joseph was a hater. He hated communism, hated drugs, hated women's lib (as it was then called), hated Susan, hated Meyers. He was stumpy and strong with acne on his face so livid it looked like someone had sprayed it on that morning. He wore Sears Roebuck short-sleeved, stain-holding shirts that reeked of the night shift. Joseph called himself conservative, but he was only that because he hadn't yet encountered a recruiter from a brownshirt operation.

Meyers wrote him off from the start. He didn't try to convert Joseph or to understand his painful home life or to contact his suppressed inner self. By indulging Joseph a little, putting his blather into cogent form for him and us, Meyers might have "gotten a good discussion going"—every teacher's dream. Instead Meyers talked with serene intelligence to Susan and anyone else who cared to volunteer and treated Joseph with subtle, and occasionally not so subtle, derision.

For Meyers thought well of himself. He wouldn't pander. And we all wondered, if unspokenly, where this guy might have gotten his considerable lode of self-esteem. Teachers, as we could have told him, were losers, out-and-out. And this one in particular wasn't strong or tough or worldly. He wore ridiculous clothes, old formal suits and that weird paper clip in his lapel; he talked like a dictionary; his accent was overcultivated, queer, absurd. He was a compendium of odd mannerisms, starting with the way he swung his right hand from the wrist laterally as he spoke. Yet he thought highly of himself. And not much at all, it wasn't difficult to see, of us. Except for Susan, whom he addressed in affectionate tones, Meyers spoke to the class with perpetual irony. He mocked us, and not always so genially, for never doing the reading, never knowing the answer, never having a thought in our heads. We were minor-league fools, his tone implied, for ignoring this chance to learn a little something before being fed live and whole to what was waiting. For our part, we sat back, let him wrangle with Joseph, and waited to see what would turn up.

One day in mid-December or so, Meyers walked in and told us to pass back our copies of *The Story of Philosophy*. Then he told us that he had some other books for us to read but that we'd have to pay for them ourselves. (Gubby Shea piped up immediately to say that this was fine with him, since he'd finished inking in the *o*'s of the Durant.) Meyers, it turned out, had asked no one's permission to do this; it just struck him as a good idea to try to get people who never picked up a book to do some reading by giving them work that might speak to their experience. At Medford High, this qualified as major educational innovation, real breakthrough thinking. And of course there were plenty of rules against using books that hadn't been approved by the school board, weren't purchased through public funding, and so on.

The books that Meyers picked were on a theme, though I had no idea of that at the time. *The Stranger, One Flew Over the Cuckoo's Nest, Group Psychology and the Analysis of the Ego, Siddhartha*: The first three were about the oppressions of conformity (among other things), the last about the Buddha's serene, fierce rebellion against it. We were all weighed down by conformity, Meyers knew. And he also knew that we, his self-selected seniors, were oppressors in our own right, passing on the ways of the system to the weaker, homelier, duller kids. These were revelations that emerged slowly for us as we talked not just about the high school and its day-to-day machinations but also about sports, sororities, circles of friends and families and what they closed out. We learned to use some unfamiliar language to talk about ourselves and so became, for a few moments at a time, strangers in our own lives, the subjects of new kinds of understanding and judgment.

I don't want to idealize this process. For the first few weeks, since virtually no one but Susan would read a book at home, we simply sat in a circle and read the pages aloud in turn. Periodically Meyers would ask a question, and usually, in the beginning, it was he who would answer it or decide finally to let it drop. One day, when we were reading *The Stranger*, Meyers asked us about solitude. What does it mean to be alone? Is it possible? What would it mean to be genuinely by oneself? Susan Rosenberg raised her hand, no doubt ready to treat us to a description of Zen meditation and its capacity to melt the ego beyond solitude into pure nothingness. But Meyers must have seen something ripple across Debbie Lauria's beautiful face. He gestured in her direction, though she hadn't volunteered.

Debbie was a high school princess, a sorority girl whose autobiography, I'd have guessed, would have translated into a graph peaking from prom to prom, with soft valleys of preparation in between. What Debbie did was run through a litany of defenses against being alone. She mentioned listening to the radio and talking on the phone, then playing the songs and conversations over in her mind, and myriad other strategies, ending, perceptively enough, with expectation, our habit of blocking out the present by waiting for things to happen in the future. But Debbie did not express herself with detachment. She said "I": "This is how I keep from being alone."

"And why," asked Meyers, "is it hard to be alone?"

"Because," Debbie answered, "I might start to think about things."

Debbie had been, up until that point, one of the Elect, pre-destined for all happiness; suddenly she had gone over to the terminally Lost. One of the great sources of grief for those who suffer inwardly is their belief that others exist who are perpetually and truly happy. From the ranks of the local happy few, Debbie had just checked out, leaving some effective hints about those she'd left behind.

The book that mattered to me wasn't *The Stranger*, which had gotten Debbie going, or Freud's book on the herd instinct (when I was writing my dissertation, a literary critical reading of Freud, my working text of *Group Psychology* was, somehow, the one that had belonged to Gubby Shea, with the *o*'s colored in to about page 20), but Kesey's *One Flew Over the Cuckoo's Nest*. It's a hard book for me to read now, with its pumped-up cartoon hero, Randall Patrick McMurphy. But at the time it was everything. I read it in a lather, running through it in about ten hours straight, then starting in again almost immediately.

But that didn't happen right off. It was probably on the fifth day of reading the book out loud in class that a chance remark Meyers made caught my attention, or what there was of it then to catch. He said that prisons, hospitals, and schools were on a continuum, controlling institutions with many of the same protocols and objectives, and that Kesey, with his bitter por-trait of the mental hospital, might be seen as commenting on all these places.

This idea, elementary as it was, smacked me with the force of revelation. Here was a writer who was not on the side of the teachers, who in fact detested them and their whole virtuous apparatus. That the book was in part crude and ugly I knew even at the time: Blacks in it are twisted sadists, the women castrators or sweet whores. But it was the antiauthoritarian part that swept me in; here was someone who found words, gorgeous, graffiti-size, and apocalyptic, for what in me had been mere inchoate impulses, dumb groans of the spirit laboring away in its own darkness.

"You can't like that book anymore," said a well-meaning, department-broken professor of English I ran into after giving a lecture in California. "You used to be able to like it, but not anymore," he said, not smugly, not knowingly, but a little wistfully. I understood what he meant, but I couldn't share the genteel sentiment. That book pulled me out of where I was. So it wasn't angelic: If you'll consent only to being saved by an angel, you may have some time to wait.

During the period when we were reading Kesey aloud and discussing him, Doug Meyers started bringing things into class. Every Friday we got some music: I remember hearing Billie Holiday, Mozart, the Incredible String Band, the Velvet Underground. The selection standard was simple—things he liked that we probably would not have heard. He also showed us art books, read a poem from time to time, and brought in friends of his to explain themselves. Meyers loved the things he offered us, but he loved them in a quirky way: He seemed to look affectionately askance at everything he cared about. What love you could find in Medford culture, where you could find it, wasn't always so easy to distinguish from the mechanism of hunger and satiety.

A panel of Students for a Democratic Society members appeared one day to debate the Vietnam War with us. (Most of us were in favor.) One February day, a group of black students burst into the room during class and announced that this was the anniversary of Malcolm X's death. Meyers looked up mildly from his place in the circle and asked the foremost of them, "And when was he born, Malcolm Little?" The young man, knew, or said he did, and gave a date. Meyers nodded and invited them to sit down and talk about politics. It was the first time I'd had an extended conversation about these things with black students, and more than a few followed. These discussions didn't stop the ongoing racial guerrilla war at Medford High, but they were something.

As time went on, word spread around the school that odd things were happening in Meyers's classroom. It was known that once, on a torpid winter day, he brought us all outside for a snowball fight. Joseph—no surprise—got it going by heaving a jagged ice chunk, caveman style, at Meyers. Meyers, who looked that day like a Mexican padre, with his long black coat and broad-brimmed black hat, responded by trying to pitch Joseph into a snowbank. Meyers was ill coordinated but determined. From where I stood, it looked as if Joseph was being attacked by a giant crow. When Joseph shook the snow off his parka and stepped up for retaliation, a bunch of us pelted him with snowballs.

As the weather warmed up, the class occasionally went outside to sit on the grass and hold discussions. This sometimes resulted in one or two of us nodding off, but Meyers didn't much care; he had most of us most of the time now. He sat cross-legged, wise-medicine-man-style, and swung his wrist and laughed, and we answered the questions he asked, because what he thought mattered probably did. It was a first, this outdoors business; no one at Medford High would have imagined doing it.

One Thursday afternoon, just as we were wrapping up a discussion of Thoreau, Meyers gave us a solemn, mischievous look, the sort of expression shrewd old rabbis are supposed to be expert in delivering, and said, "There's been some doubt expressed about our going outside." Then he told a story. In the faculty cafeteria, with plenty of the other teachers milling around, Meyers had been approached by Dandy Dan O'Mara, the submaster, the disciplinarian. O'Mara had the sly bullying style of a hard Irish cop. He had a barroom face, red nose, watery eyes, the hands of someone who worked for a living. He was stepping up to put Meyers in his place.

O'Mara got rapidly to the point. What would happen, he'd asked Meyers, if everyone held class outside? Now, this was familiar stuff to us all. O'Mara's question came out of that grand conceptual bag that also contained lines like "Did you bring gum for everyone?" and "Would you like to share that note with the whole class?" O'Mara was trying to treat Meyers like a student, like one of us, and in front of his colleagues. At Medford High, there were two tribes, us and them. Meyers had defied the authorities; clearly he had become one of *them*, a student, of no use or interest whatever. But in fact Meyers was of no particular clan but his own, the tribe of rootless, free-speculating readers and talkers and writers who owe allegiance first to a pile of books that they've loved, and then, only secondly, to other things.

O'Mara did not know this. Nor did he know that Meyers, however diminutive, mild, and Mandarinly self-effacing, thought himself something of a big deal. So O'Mara would not have been prepared when Meyers drew an easy breath and did what every high school kid would like to do when confronted with this sort of bullying. He didn't fight it, didn't stand on his dignity. He simply ran with it. What if everyone held class outside on sunny days? Suppose that happened? And from there, Meyers went on to draw a picture of life at Medford High School—a picture that had people outside on the vast lawn talking away about books and ideas and one thing and another, hanging out, being lazy and being absorbed, thinking hard from time to time, and reveling in the spring. It was Woodstock and Socrates' agora fused, and Meyers spun it out for us, just as he had for O'Mara. What if that happened, he asked us (and the submaster)? How tragic would it be?

This vision of the renovated school took a long time to unfold, and it had something like a musical form, ebbing and rising, threading back through major themes and secondary motifs. And in my mind's eye, I could see O'Mara wilting, growing too small for his wrinkled, sad clothes. He would soon know, as we did, that Meyers could produce plenty more of this (he was the most eloquent man I'd met) and that it was time to cut and run. What struck me about the performance (and I believed Meyers's rendition of it, word for word—he was unfailingly, often unflatteringly honest) was that it was done with words alone, nothing equivalent to the body blows Kesey's R.P. McMurphy specializes in.

We went outside whenever we chose to after that. It was very odd: I had been at Medford High for three years, and I had never seen O'Mara's side lose a round. I'd seen a kid from the city's preeminent street gang, the South Medford Bears, spit in a teacher's face, but soon enough the police wagon was there and the big boy was trussed and bawling and on the way to jail. After class was over on the day that Meyers told us the O'Mara story, John Aquino, the quarterback of the football team and very little in line with the stereotype, said to me, "You know, Meyers can really be an asshole when he wants to be." In Medford, there were fifty intonations you could apply to the word *asshole*. Spun right, the word constituted high praise.

O'Mara was a broad target. America was in crisis then; people were assuming intense allegorical identities—pig, peacenik, hawk, dove. O'Mara had turned into an ugly monolith, at least in our eyes. In Asia, the Vietcong were making fools of his spiritual brethren, Johnson, Westmoreland, McNamara, and the rest. His sort was on the run. In the next few years it would get even worse for them. But Meyers, for his part, hadn't treated O'Mara as among the lost, even though he probably had it coming. Instead he'd invited him to a party, an outdoor extravaganza. At the time, O'Mara surely couldn't discern the invitation in Meyers's extended aria, but who knows what he might have seen later on as he turned it all over in his mind.

That year of teaching was the last for Doug Meyers. He got married, went to law school, and, I heard, eventually moved to Maine, where he could pursue a life a little akin to the one Thoreau, his longtime idol, managed to lead during his stay at Walden. I haven't seen Meyers in about twenty-five years. But I do carry around with me the strong sense that the party he invited us to, me and Carla and Gubby and Michael de Leo and Dandy Dan O'Mara (but not Joseph, no, not everyone, quite), is still a live possibility. Sometimes I even stumble on an installment of it, or help make one.

I had great teachers after Doug Meyers, some of the world's most famous in fact, but I never met his equal. What I liked most about him, I suppose, was that for all the minor miracle of what he accomplished with us, he was no missionary: He served us but also himself. He got what he wanted out of Medford High, which was a chance to affront his spiritual enemies, though with some generosity, and to make younger people care about the sorts of things he cared about, to pull them out of their parents' orbit and into his. All good teaching entails some kidnapping; there's a touch of malice involved.

As well as some sorrow. Good teachers have many motivations, but I suspect that loneliness is often one of them. You need a small group, a coterie, to talk to; unable to find it in the larger world, you try to create it in the smaller sphere of a classroom. Meyers, who seemed at times a little lost in his life, a brilliant orphan, did something like that with us. (When he saw the material he had to work with on that first day, he must have been on the verge of stepping out the window.) Whatever his motives, part of what I admired about him was his streak of arrogance. His goodness had some edge to it.

It would be a mistake to believe that what Meyers taught about teaching was that always and until the end of time you should draw the chairs into a circle, read pop-cult marvels like *Cuckoo's Nest*, and apply them directly to the situation at hand. No, Meyers taught something else entirely. When I call him to mind in that long black padre coat, he reminds me of Groucho Marx in *Horse Feathers*, duck-walking at top throttle back and forth in front of a whole congress of professors, singing out his Marxian ditty with the gorgeous refrain, "Whatever it is, I'm against it!"

What Meyers taught—or at least what I gleaned from him— is that anything that's been successfully institutionalized, however rebellious it may seem or however virtuous, is stifling. What's called subversion only lasts for an instant in a school or a hospital or a home; it's quickly swept up to become part of the protocol, an element in "the way we do things around here." At the time, Kesey and Camus collided well enough with the dead protocols of Medford High, but now, for all I know, they fit in fine—maybe alienation has become standard issue. What to do then? When Bacchus is ascendant, when all the world is a pop-cult blast, then maybe you become a high priest of Apollo, with his hard graces. Teachers, freelance spirit healers that they are or ought to be, make a diagnosis, pour out a cure or two, then see what happens. Or so Meyers did with us.

Such teaching incites friction. Many students, the successes in particular, resent it and respond with civil venom. And teachers, undercompensated as they usually are, often yearn for some adulation to balance the books. It's tough to be both broke and unloved.

"Whenever others agree with me," the sublime Oscar Wilde said, "I know that I must be wrong." When students love you from day one, when you succeed too fast, chances are that Wilde's dictum applies. And when the world does eventually come around to your way of thinking, maybe then it's time to deliver your premises a salutary whack: "Whatever it is," chants Groucho from the wings, "I'm against it."

This approach isn't without its costs. One pays for the kind of mental exhilaration that Meyers initiated. One pays in self-doubt and isolation, in the suspicion that what seems to be true resistance is merely a perverse substitute for genuine talent, a cheap way of having something to say. Meyers's path, so appealing in its first steps, separated me from my family and cut me loose from religion. It sent me adrift beyond the world bordered by TV and piety and common sense. One step down that road followed another, and now I probably could not turn around if I wished to.

Still, the image I most often hit on when I think about Meyers glows brightly enough. It's late spring, a gloomy dead day. He's brought in a record by the Incredible String Band. He's at the back of the room standing beside the beat-up phonograph. I dislike the record and open my book, *The Autobiography of Malcolm X*, which has not been assigned in any class, and disappear into it. Meyers cranks the music a little louder. I keep reading. But then, curious, I raise my head. The racket of the String Band floods in. And there in the back of the room, Meyers is dancing away. He's a so-so dancer at best, stiff and arrhythmic. Not until I saw Bob Dylan in concert did I ever see anyone dance as self-consciously. Yet it struck me that this was probably the first time anyone had ever danced in this building. The air was so heavy with gray institutional weight: I can't imagine that anyone but Meyers could have pulled it off.

But here he was, dancing away. It was like a few good new words coming into the language, some strokes of light rendered by a painter for the first time, though with an unsteady enough hand. Meyers had scored a benevolent victory over the place. (You could say he'd beaten Medford High at its own game, but really he'd shown it a new one.) He had a right to a little celebration.

THE PINK FLOYD NIGHT SCHOOL

S O, WHAT ARE you doing after graduation?"
In the spring of my last year in college I posed that question to at least a dozen fellow graduates-to-be at my little out-of-the-way school in Vermont. The answers they gave me were satisfying in the extreme: not very much, just kick back, hang out, look things over, take it slow. It was 1974. That's what you were supposed to say.

My classmates weren't, strictly speaking, telling the truth. They were, one might even say, lying outrageously. By graduation day, it was clear that most of my contemporaries would be trotting off to law school and graduate school and to cool and unusual internships in New York and San Francisco.

But I did take it slow. After graduation, I spent five years wandering around doing nothing—or getting as close to it as I could manage. I was a cab driver, an obsessed moviegoer, a wanderer in the mountains of Colorado, a teacher at a crazy grand hippie school in Vermont, the manager of a movie house (who didn't do much managing), a crewman on a ship, and a doorman at a disco.

The most memorable job of all, though, was a gig on the stage crew for a rock production company that worked Jersey City. We did our shows at Roosevelt Stadium, a grungy behemoth that could hold sixty thousand, counting seats on the grass. I humped amps out of the trucks and onto the stage; six or so hours later I humped them back. I did it for the Grateful Dead and Alice Cooper and the Allman Brothers and Crosby, Stills & Nash on the night that Richard Nixon resigned. But the most memorable night of that most memorable job was the night of Pink Floyd.

Pink Floyd demanded a certain quality of sound. They wanted their amps stacked high, not just onstage, where they were so broad and tall and forbidding that they looked like a barricade in the Paris Commune. They also wanted amp clusters at three highly elevated points around the stadium, and I spent the morning lugging huge blocks of wood and circuitry up and up and up the stairs of the decayed old bowl.

There was one other assignment: installing and inflating a parachute-like white silken canopy roof that Pink Floyd required over the stage. It took about six hours to get the thing up and in position. We were told that this was the first use of the canopy. Pink's guys had some blueprints, but those turned out not to be of much use. Eventually the roof did rise and inflate by means of a lot of spontaneous knot tying and strategic rope tangling.

Pink Floyd went on at about ten that night, but the amp clusters that we'd expended all that servile sweat to build didn't work—Jersey City being Jersey City, people had sat on them, kicked them, or cut the cords. So Pink made its noise, the towers stayed mute, the mob flicked on lighters at the end, and then we spent three hours breaking the amps down and loading the truck. We felt we'd wasted our time on the speakers up high on the stadium steps, so we refused to go after them. After some sharp words, Pink's guys had to scramble up and retrieve them.

There was, for the record, almost always tension between the roadies and the stage crew. One time, at a show by (if memory serves) Queen, their five roadies got into a brawl with a dozen of our stage-crew guys; then the house security, mostly Jersey bikers and black-belt karate devotees, heard the noise and jumped in. The roadies held on for a while, but finally they saw it was a lost cause. One of them grabbed a case of champagne from the truck cab and opened a bottle and passed it around—all became drunk and happy.

Pink's road manager wanted the inflatable canopy brought down gently, then folded and packed securely in its wooden boxes. The problem was that the thing was full of helium and no one knew where the release valve was; we'd also secured it to the stage with so many knots of such foolish intricacy that their disentanglement would have given a gang of sailors pause. Everyone was tired. Those once intoxicated were no longer. It was four A.M. and time to go home.

An hour went into concocting strategies to get the floating pillowy roof down. It became a regular seminar. Then came Timmy our crew chief, who looked like a good-natured Viking captain and who defended the integrity of his stage crew at every turn, even going so far as to have screamed at Stevie Nicks, who was yelling at me for having dropped a guitar case, that he was the only one who had the right to holler at Edmundson. Faced with the Pink Floyd roof crisis, Timmy did what he always could be counted on to do in critical circumstances, which is to say, he did something.

Timmy walked softly to a corner of the stage, reached into his pocket, removed a buck knife, and with it began to saw one of the ropes attaching the holy celestial roof to the earth. Three or four of us, his minions, did the same. "Hey, what are you doing?" wailed Pink's head roadie. "I'll smash your—" Only then did he realize that Timmy had a knife in his hand, and that most of the rest of us did, too. In the space of a few minutes, we sawed through the ropes.

There came a great sighing noise as the last thick cord broke apart. For a moment there was nothing; for another moment, more of the same.

Then the canopy rose into the air and began to float away, like a gorgeous cloud, white and soft. The sun at that moment burst above the horizon and the silk bloomed into a soft crimson tinge. Timmy started to laugh a big beer-bellied laugh. We all joined. Even Pink's guys did. We were like little kids on the last day of school. We stood on the naked stage, watching the silk roof go up and out, wafting over the Atlantic. Some of us waved.

"So, what are you doing after graduation?" Thirty-five years later, a college teacher, I ask my students the old question. They aren't inclined to dissimulate now. The culture is on their side when they tell me about law school and med school and higher degrees in journalism and business, or when they talk about a research grant in China or a well-paying gig teaching English in Japan.

I'm impressed, sure, but I'm worried about them too. Aren't they deciding too soon? Shouldn't they hang out a little, learn to take it slow? I can't help it. I flash on that canopy of white silk floating out into the void. I can see it as though it were still there. I want to point up to it. I'd like for all my students to see it, too.

FELLOW TEACHERS

A WORD TO THE NEW
HUMANITIES PROFESSOR

WELCOME TO THE university—marvelous to have you
here. Congratulations on your appointment to assistant
professor! A position like yours is hard to get—but you know
that. But perhaps what you don't know is this: Such a position
is even harder to keep. You've already achieved a great deal and
maybe you've done that by accepting no one's counsel but your
own. If so, fine. But maybe a word of assistance and a word or
two of warning might be helpful. So—if you like—listen.

If success is what you crave, if prosperity and esteem, tenure,
preferment, and promotion are what you desire—and who
does not?—then you might begin by studying your admissions-
office brochure, the pictorial ad for your school. Whatever its
overt designs, this book is also a manual for pedagogical success, a discreet academic version of *The Book of the Courtier.*

In these brochures, these ads, two photographic genres pre-
dominate. One genre is a version of romance; its subject is easy
pleasure, the world as the readers wish it to be. Students are
arrayed in a conversational garland, lounging on well-tended
grass. The sun smiles down. They are talking freely, savoring

one another's company. If there are books on hand, they've been tossed carelessly aside. This is not about dialogue or dialectic, not about effort. These students are in the Bower of Bliss, intoxicated by each other's presences, relaxed, happy, stress-free.

The other sort of photograph is quite different. In this genre, which is a version of Futuristic Utopian, a group of students presses tightly in on a large, forbidding piece of electronic equipment. It is high-tech, high-powered, and, to you probably, completely mysterious. This picture is not about good times. Serious business is unfolding. A thrill of purposeful engagement rises from the page.

Generally missing from both sorts of pictures are intrusive adults, professorial types, who might inhibit the fun in the first kind of picture or undermine the students' pure self-motivation in the second. What is missing from both these sorts of photographs, to put it bluntly, is you, the professor. And in this there is a valuable lesson. Don't let it be lost.

Pleasure and high-powered training: The sweetly meandering discussion and the high-tech initiation, these are the things a student can now expect, in fact demand, from an American college. You, invisible, self-abnegating, ever agreeable, will provide these commodities. You will provide them or—more than likely—you will find yourself another line of work.

How does a contemporary humanities professor abet the pursuit of enjoyment?

First of all, he must contrive to present all course material in an agreeable manner. Reading assignments should be slight: For one semester, three or four "long" books, that is, books of more than 250 pages, will more than do. The instructor must understand that those students who actually read the books will for the most part do so glancingly. In high school they have learned to budget their time, which means they have learned to skim, extracting "the main points." The teacher should not be surprised to see that those books that *have been* opened are streaked occasionally with highlighter. Those who have "read" an assigned novel will, in general, know who the main characters are and what, in broad terms, has come to pass.

But they will not at all object to being reminded of these things, and those who have decided not to crack the book will believe it to be the professor's responsibility—what else is she being paid for?—to tell them in amusing detail what went on inside. Some students believe it is up to the teacher to describe the book so appealingly (to advertise it, in short) that later in life, given leisure, they might have a look.

The summary and description should be carried on in a diverting way. There ought to be copious reference to analogous themes and plots in recent popular culture. Jokes ought to be offered at the expense of at least some of the characters, preferably all. The author, no matter how distinguished, should be referred to with no more veneration than attachés to the creator of a reasonably successful TV sitcom. In no event should the instructor hint that the author or the characters in the book are in any way superior to the students who have condescended to encounter them.

Students should be assured continually that by virtue of living later in time than the author, they naturally know a great deal more than he possibly could. Sometimes authors will anticipate, or dimly guess at, a piece of contemporary wisdom, in which case they are to be gently congratulated. Generally, authors whose works appeared more than two decades ago are caught up in errors endemic to their times and need to be brought up short. The teacher should give the students every chance to do so. If this process can be effected with the aid of an up-to-date theoretical vocabulary, then all the better.

The proper atmosphere for an enjoyable classroom is relaxed and cool. The teacher should never get exercised about anything, under pain of being written off as a buffoon. Nor should she create an atmosphere of vital contention where students lose their composure, speak out, become passionate, express their deeper thoughts and fears, or do anything else that will, later on, cause them embarrassment. Embarrassment is the worst thing that can befall one; it must be avoided at whatever cost.

It is important here to distinguish being cool from being ironic. Cool is a state of superiority maintained at a consistent level. It is an attitude. Cool does not fluctuate. It is democratic and egalitarian in that it meets all phenomena with the same measure of blank detachment. It is programmatic and readily assumed.

Irony is something different. To be ironic is to express skepticism about this or that outside phenomenon, and also—at times— about one's own powers of apprehension and judgment. Cool never undermines the self; it is directed outward. Irony can be self-subverting. It can demonstrate lack of self-esteem, and is therefore to be avoided.

Irony is also inconsistent, in that it relies on judgment. The ironist is more skeptical about some things than others and communicates as much. Irony, by virtue of being selective, is elitist. Irony can also hurt people's feelings. One must never be ironic in front of students because some of them will not understand the application of the irony. They will become confused and possibly offended. Irony can also make things unclear. One is bound as a professor to be as clear as possible at all times.

Satire—that is to say, protracted irony—is pure poison; no

customer-respecting professor should ever conceive of indulging in it.

Cool, on the other hand, is okay. Being cool is a sign of confidence. Being cool indicates that one has made all of the judgments that matter in life and made them correctly. Cool is consistent, steady, and reliable, where irony is uncertain, fluctuating, and insecure. Cool is irony that has become frozen over time.

The teacher should be friendly, though not overly intimate; she should be concerned but not intrusive. She should be in her office as many hours per week as possible. Office availability shows dedication and indicates that the student is getting a good value for his dollars. But the student almost never visits the office. One-on-one conversation can sometimes drift toward disturbing topics—why I'm desperate to transfer to the commerce school, although all of my favorite classes are in the arts; why my sorority has never had a black member; why I have to take these pills so as not to become disablingly depressed. Such topics can make the student uncomfortable. Comfort is all.

E-mail is the preferred form of communication. With e-mail, there is more control. The conversation is in no danger of jumping the rails. One can ask one's own businesslike questions; one can set the tone. The professor should answer e-mail communications within three hours' time. She should not refer the student to this or that book but answer personally, from her own knowledge, with the fewest necessary number of words.

The professor should continually make self-mocking references to her authority and her stock of learning. She should indicate that all the time she has spent acquiring her knowledge may have been wasted, given new developments, such as the

Internet, which have changed everything, making much of the past irrelevant. The professor should refer with a respect that stops tastefully short of sycophancy to the large stock of pop-culture knowledge that all of her students possess simply by virtue of having grown up with unparalleled access to TV, movies, and recorded music. She should compliment their remarkable "visual literacy" from time to time. She should use this term—which generally refers to such feats as identifying the TV shows parodied in a given *Simpsons* episode—in rebutting Philistines from outside the academy who claim that many students are now willfully nonliterate, don't read and don't want to.

In choosing what to teach, the professor should meet students halfway. He should realize that he has his culture, which may feature, let us say, the novels of Jane Austen and Charles Dickens; the poetry of Emily Dickinson and Walt Whitman; the historical works of Frances Parkman and Edward Gibbon; the psychoanalysis of Freud; the social thought of Plato, Jefferson, Marx, and Arendt; and the jazz of Coltrane. But students have their culture, too. Insofar as he is in a position to do so, he should offer—it would be presumptuous to say "teach"—courses in the more demotic, vital, and diverse popular culture that the students endorse.

In doing so, it is important that he not be chauvinistic. He must take seriously the possibility that another's experience with Anne Rice might be as vitally nourishing as his own experience with Emily Dickinson. He must consider the possibility that Dickinson, with her difficulty, helps sustain an elitist high culture and that reading and teaching her reaffirms class divisions, while Rice, whose accounts of sadomasochistic and pedophilic bliss are available to all, moves us toward equality. He must, in short, learn as much as possible from his students.

He must take very seriously (but never quite so far as to articulate) the central lesson that his students have to instill: that he is a service provider, not entirely unlike the dentist, the stockbroker (before online trading), and the man who comes to clean the pool. He must remember that he works for them, and that they, all things considered, are very indulgent bosses, but that he ought not to forget how the rolls are buttered and by whom.

As to grades, he should understand that students care nothing about them. They say this repeatedly, in e-mails, and in his office, when they come, so it must be so. But this established truth needs elaboration. Students do not care about grades as long as certain protocols are observed. The first of these protocols is what one might call the default standard. The default standard dictates that if a student comes periodically to class, does some self-determined quotient of the reading, and hands in a semblance of every assignment, the grade will be a B-plus. All other grades are A's.

This sort of grading, which may appear unjustifiably high to outsiders, is pedagogically useful in that it keeps the students happily engaged and does not discourage them (students now are easily discouraged). It also induces them to write positive course evaluations. Negative course evaluations can have an unfortunate effect on a professor's career. Negative course evaluations that include charges of, say, racism or sexism, no matter how imaginary, can have disastrous effects. It is best to follow the grading policies that have been laid down, informally, by the students. Pay lip service to administrators' calls for tightening grades, but understand who, in this instance, the real policy makers are.

If you follow this advice, elaborating and extending it as you see the need, you will be likely to produce the right quotient of enjoyment to succeed as a current professor of humanities. But enjoyment production is only half of your job. For students are aware that college is also serious business. There is a time for relaxation, but there is also a time to set to work.

Besides creating pleasure, you must also help the student to acquire skills that he or she can turn to profit in the future. You are a facilitator—not a "sage on the stage" but a "guide on the side." You must teach—no, rather, you must help the students to acquire—skills in communication, critical thinking, technology, and teamwork. Without these skills, it is unlikely that anyone can be truly successful in tomorrow's high-stress, high-competition world. Without these skills, a person cannot call him- or herself truly educated.

As a communications facilitator, you will be compelled to work very hard. Your comments on all written products submitted by students must be copious. The students and their families are paying good money, and it is here that they want to see you earn it. It is important that your comments be clear, precise, and practical. Students need to know what they have to do in order to improve as communicators. Note every error; correct every mistake in grammar, spelling, and punctuation. When an argument is not well structured or when a sentence is ambiguous, show the student how to remedy the problem. Rewrite the relevant passages if need be.

You must understand that writing is a form of technology the function of which is to transfer information from one person to another, or one site to another. Nothing must be lost in the transfer. It is not your function to comment on the ideas per se. Students' ideas are their own and they have a personal validity. You have no right to judge them. What you can judge is skill at expression and presentation. A paper arguing that Hamlet and Iago are actually brothers separated at birth may seem to you misguided. This fact is irrelevant. The issue for you to ponder is whether the essay is well written, presents its points lucidly, and is organized along coherent lines. To succeed in life, a person needs to know how to get his ideas across. You are instrumental in helping students to develop this capacity.

Lack of clarity that comes from technical inability is something that you must remedy. But there are other kinds of occlusion that you also need to help students avoid. Though a metaphor can sometimes make things more understandable, the general tendency of metaphor is to produce multiple meanings, and those meanings lead to imprecision, and accordingly to confusion. It is a good idea to help students purge their writing of metaphors, similes, and other potentially mystifying figures of speech. Poetic writing, which was once thought to enrich experience by unfolding more and more layers of meaning and possibility, is now understood to be counterproductive.

Like irony, metaphor can make matters confusing and cause people to feel uncomfortable. Metaphor and irony can make students feel stupid and, at a good college, where students have high SAT scores, no one can accurately be described as stupid. Metaphor, like irony, can contribute to self-esteem problems. But once one has realized that the purpose of writing is to convey information and not to unfold or discover the life of the inner self, or to create original visions of the world (we now know that there is no such thing as originality), then problems associated with metaphor and other mannered forms of writing tend to disappear.

As everyone now realizes, the computer is the most significant invention in the history of humankind. Students who do not master its intricacies are destined for a life of shame, poverty, and neglect. Every course you teach should be computer oriented. Computers are excellent research tools, and so your students should do a lot of research. If you are studying a poem by Blake like "The Chimney Sweeper," which depicts the debasement and exploitation of young boys whose lot, it's been said, is not altogether unlike the lot of many children now living in American inner cities, you should charge your students with using the computer to compile as much interesting information about the poem as they can. They can find articles about chimney sweepers from 1790s newspapers; contemporary pictures and engravings that depict these unfortunate little creatures; critical articles that interpret the poem in a seemingly endless variety of equally valid and interesting ways; biographical information about Blake, with hints about events in his own boyhood that would have made chimney sweepers a special interest; portraits of the author at various stages of his life; maps of Blake's London. Together the class can create a Blake–Chimney Sweeper website: www.blakesweeper.edu.

Instead of spending class time wondering what the poem might mean, and what application it might have to present-day experience—activities that can produce only disagreement and are probably futile anyway since there is no truth about literary works, just interpretations—students can compile information about the poem. They can set the poem in its historical and critical context, showing first how the poem is the product of the past and implicitly how it really has nothing to do with the enlightened present except as an artful curiosity; and second how, given the number of ideas about it already available, adding more thoughts would be superfluous.

Computers have made everything much easier in life, chiefly because you can buy anything you want using them and get it delivered almost immediately. But the Internet is also good because it erases the old puzzlement about the differences among wisdom, knowledge, and information. Everything that can be accessed online is equal to everything else. No piece of data is intrinsically more important or more profound than any other. Therefore, there really is no more wisdom; there is no more knowledge; there is only information. Nothing has to be taken as a challenge or an affront to what one currently knows and values. And that fact can be very freeing.

At one time, ill-natured people used to say that excessive use of certain kinds of technology, and uncritical celebration of it, could be bad for you. These people—many of whom belonged to something called the Frankfurt School, had to flee Hitler's Germany, and thus had developed a resentful attitude toward life—said that technology could make you someone who felt possessed with godlike powers. If you spent too much time manipulating objects, these people suggested, you could begin treating people as though they were objects, too.

They felt that technology gave you an abstract and utilitarian relation to life, and that instead of seeing rocks and flowers and trees, you began seeing foundation material, interior decor, and timber. They thought that technology could make you cold and unsympathetic to the living world. Another man, a philosopher who wrote earlier in this century and was taken to be very gifted but who discredited his work by becoming a Nazi, talked about how technology could make one forget the strangeness of Being. Technology, as he saw it, tended to separate us from wonder and from questions like "Why is there something instead of nothing at all?" But things have changed. With the coming of the computer, most of us have stopped worrying about these issues and nothing really bad has happened. It seems clear that we did not need to be concerned about them and that the resentful men and women, probably because of their traumatic life experiences, had it wrong.

Another thing that students need to acquire are skills in group interaction. It is important that you break your students into groups as much as possible and let them engage in the uninhibited exchange of ideas, their ideas. As everyone now knows, the students have within them the answers to all questions that matter; they merely need a supportive and nonjudgmental environment for their thoughts to emerge. (Plato, it turns out, was right when he endorsed anamnesis, the view that we all knew the truth in a prior life but that, on being born, forget it, so that we need not so much to be informed as to be reminded. Or at least Plato was right about American students of the present.) It is important that you do not intrude on these discussions with your sophisticated terms and your experienced perspective. Keep in mind: Your views may be flawed. And the students, given time, will do productive work on their own.

But of course answers are not really the point. The point is learning to work together and to get along. High grades should go to the people who cooperate best, no matter what you, with your biases, might think about the eventual product. In the future, it may be very important to be able to please and even placate the group. Learning how to submit your so-called individuality to a collective may be a good professional skill and could be a good survival skill as well.

Pleasure and training: These are the things that you offer, and the more modestly and unobtrusively you do so, the better. If you do your job well, you will get the appreciation you deserve. Students in coming years will write you letters about their prosperity and happiness and about how much you did to facilitate them. They will thank you for your patience and your ability to convey important skills. They will praise your powers of communication. They will say that they never could have done it without you, and you will feel both grateful and exalted.

But the road will not always be smooth. Sometimes you will encounter a student who offers a particular challenge, and you must be ready for it. This is the sort of student who comes to college with mistaken expectations. Perhaps he has spent some time reading about Socrates, who asked annoying, self-important questions about everything; or perhaps in high school he had a teacher who encouraged her students to ask about what bearing the things they were reading might have on their lives.

This student comes to college expecting more of the Socrates business. He doesn't care all that much about skills and wants to know whether you think his ideas are true or not. He doesn't write all that badly, but often he sinks into needless ambiguity and confusion. He talks a lot in class. One time, a colleague of yours sees him in the library with a book open. He is laughing his head off. Another time he is seen reading the newspaper and crying. Why, your colleague asks, would anyone read the front page of a newspaper and weep?

This student works hard; in fact he works too hard. He's in your office all the time asking bothersome questions wanting to know the names of fresh books to read, as though the syllabus isn't enough. He writes stories and other things that are not assigned. He plays in a band.

He is also cynical. He laughs at you and others when you talk about cultivating skills that will land good jobs. He mocks the whole idea of training. He says that most of the Internet looks like an electronic shopping mall to him. He says that he has no idea what he wants to do in life; he's uncertain what way of living is the best. He's confused about what goodness really is, who possesses it, and how it might be acquired. He'll be happy to talk about job skills, he says, but only after he's got these questions answered, or at least is on the way to answering them. Though he often says abrupt and potentially embarrassing things to them, many of the other students seem to like him.

It's important to use patience when dealing with such students. They are a challenge, certainly, but they can also be very rewarding. Guiding them from their current confusions onto a better path can provide one of the strongest professional satisfactions there is.

One of the difficulties in doing so, one must confess, is the kind of feelings these students can provoke in you, the teacher. They often bring on a very powerful nostalgia. They take you back to a time before graduate school when you too perhaps thought that certain great works of art and reflection could guide you to a new sort of self. They make you recall when you thought that it might be worthwhile to try to become more like this or that hero or thinker you encountered in a book. These students take you back to a very impassioned time, to be sure. But it was also a turbulent and unproductive time. You know better now, and with your guidance so will this wayward, gifted student. This student needs you. He needs your wisdom and experience. He needs you to put him on one of the straighter, more satisfying roads.

Despite his apparent confidence, and even occasional bursts of what appears to be joy, this is really a troubled individual. Deep in his heart he does not want to be as he is. On some level he wants to change. For to be someone who sits in the library, in public, reading a common everyday newspaper with tears flowing down his cheeks, what kind of life is that? What kind of future could such behavior, uncorrected, ever prepare him for?

AGAINST READINGS

IF I COULD make one wish for the members of my profession—college and university professors of literature— I would wish that for one year, two, three, or five, we give up readings. By a reading, I mean the application of an analytical vocabulary—Marx's, Freud's, Foucault's, Derrida's, or whoever's—to describe and (usually) judge a work of literary art. I wish that we'd declare a moratorium on readings. I wish that we'd give readings a rest.

This wish will strike most academic literary critics and perhaps others as well as—let me put it politely—counterintuitive. Readings, many think, are what we do. Readings are what literary criticism is all about. They are the bread and butter of the profession. Through readings we write our books; through readings we teach our students. And if there were no more readings, what would we have left to do? Wouldn't we have to close our classroom doors, shut down our office computers, and go home? The end of readings, presumably, would mean the end of our profession.

So let me try to explain what I have in mind. For it seems to me that if we kicked our addiction to readings, our profession would actually be stronger and more influential, our teaching would improve, and there would be more good books of literary criticism to be written and accordingly more to be read.

In my view—a view informed by, among others, William Blake, Ralph Waldo Emerson, and Matthew Arnold—the best way to think of a literary education is as a great second chance. We all get socialized once. We spend the first years of our lives learning the usages of our families, our neighborhoods, our religions, our schools, and our nations. We come to an understanding of what's expected: We come to see what the world takes to be good and bad, right and wrong. We figure out ways to square the ethics of our church with the ethics of our neighborhood— they aren't always the same, but one reason that religions survive and thrive is that they can enter into productive commerce with the values present in other spheres of life. Kids go to primary school so that they can learn their ABCs and math facts, certainly. But they also go to be socialized: They go to acquire a set of more or less public values. Then it's up to them (and their parents) to square those values with the home truths they've acquired in their families. Socialization isn't a simple process, but when it works well, it can produce individuals who thrive in themselves and either do no harm to others or make a genuine contribution to society at large.

But primary socialization doesn't work for everyone. There are always people—how many it's tough to know, but surely a minority—who don't see their own natures fully reflected in the values that they're supposed to inherit or assume. They feel out of joint with their times. The gay kid who grows up in a family that thinks homosexuality is a sin. The young guy with a potent individualist streak who can't bear the drippy collectivism foisted on him by his ex-hippie parents and his purportedly progressive school. The girl who is supposed to be a chip off the old legal block and sit someday on the Supreme Court but only wants to draw and paint; the guy destined (in his mom's heart) for Princeton who's born to be a carpenter and has no real worldly ambitions, no matter how often he's upbraided.

To be young is often to know—or to sense—what others have in mind for you and not to like it. But what is harder for a person who has gone unhappily through the first rites of passage into the tribe is to know how to replace the values she's had imposed on her with something better. She's learned a lot of socially sanctioned languages, and still none of them are hers. But are there any that truly might be? Is there something she might be or do in the world that's truly in keeping with the insistent but often speechless self that presses forward internally?

This, I think, is where literature can come in—as can all of the other arts and in some measure the sciences, too. By venturing into what Arnold called "the best that has been known and thought," a young person has the chance to discover new vital possibilities. Such a person sees that there are other ways of looking at the world and other ways of being in the world than the ones that she's inherited from her family and culture. She sees, with Emily Dickinson, that a complex, often frayed, often humorous dialogue with God *must* be at the center of her life; she sees with Charles Dickens that humane decency is the highest of human values and understands that her happiness will come from shrewdly serving others; she likes the sound of Blake and—I don't know—forms a better rock band than the ones we've been hearing for the last decade and more; he seconds Johnson and Burke and becomes a conservative, in his way twice wiser than NPR-addicted, Prius-proselytizing Mom and Dad.

In short, the student reads and feels that sensation that Emerson describes so well at the beginning of "Self-Reliance": "In every work of genius we recognize our own rejected thoughts: they come back to us with a certain alienated majesty." The truth of what we're best fit to do is latent in all of us, Emerson suggests, and I think this to be right. But it's also true that we, and society, too, have plenty of tricks for keeping that most important kind of knowledge out of reach. Society seems to have a vested interest in telling us what we should do and be. But often its interpretation of us—fed through teachers and guidance officers and priests and ministers and even through our loving parents—is simply wrong. When we feel—as Longinus said we will in the presence of the sublime—that we have created what in fact we've only heard, then it's time to hearken with particular attention and see how this startling utterance might be beckoning us to think, or speak, or even to live differently.

Everyone who teaches literature has probably had at least one such golden moment. I mean the moment where, reading casually or reading intently, being lazy or being responsive, one is shocked into recognition. "Yes," one says, "that's the way it really is." Then, often, a rather antinomian utterance comes: "They say it's not so, but I know it is. I always have."

One of my own such moments occurred reading *The Autobiography of Malcolm X*—something I've mentioned before, but that seems to me well worth elaborating on. It didn't really figure: That shouldn't have been *the* book (as it was at least for a little while) for a white, Irish Catholic kid growing up outside of Boston. What Malcolm had to say about race resonated with me: There was a low-grade race war in my school at the time, and he changed my thoughts about it pretty directly. In sum, I began to see how scary it must be to be black in America, to be in real danger much of the time from white officials and white cops and white kids (kids not altogether unlike me and my pals).

But what really struck me in that book, oddly enough, was Malcolm's hunger for learning. By now nearly everyone knows the story of how Malcolm, in prison, found himself unfit for the arguments that proliferated in the prison yard (or at least one quadrant of it) and took in all subjects under the moon and sun: race, sex, politics, history. He had opinions, but he couldn't back them up. He had almost no facts in his mental files. The answer was simple: He needed to start reading. So he loaded his cell with meaty works from the prison library. But of course smart as the then Malcolm Little was, he hadn't much formal education and the books were loaded with words he didn't understand, placed like land mines in every paragraph. He looked them up in the dictionary, but there were simply too many of them. In the process of running around in the dictionary, he'd forget what the paragraph at hand was supposed to be about.

But this didn't induce him to give up. Instead, Malcolm sat down with a dictionary and a notebook and began copying down the dictionary—starting maybe with *aardvark*—and moving on down the line. It took a while and it wasn't the most scintillating of pastimes, but when it was over, Malcolm Little could read.

And he read ferociously. The whole world of thought came into being for him: history, philosophy, literature, science. He vowed then that he would be a reader for the rest of his life, a learner; and in time he would vow to use his book-won knowledge, along with a considerable quotient of street smarts, to help himself through life and to do what he could for his people. In the beginning, doing what he could for black people meant bedeviling the white man; in time, it meant doing his part to serve all of humanity.

I was thrilled to read this. It turned out that I—despite being about as impatient with formal schooling as Malcolm was—had some intellectual aspirations, too. I was curious about things, after my fashion. Malcolm was black, I was white: Still, my seventeen-year-old self saw him as someone I could, in certain regards, try to emulate. I could read to satisfy my thirst for knowledge; I could use what I learned to make my life a little better, and maybe help some other people along the way. It was an unlikely conversion experience, maybe, but ultimately that's what it was.

I suspect that virtually everyone who teaches literature has had such an experience, and maybe more than one. They've read Emerson or Orwell or Derrida or Woolf and have been moved to change the way they do what they do—or they've chosen another way of life altogether. And even if they don't change, they've had the chance to have their fundamental values challenged. Sometimes a true literary education appears to leave a student where he was at the beginning. But that state is only apparent. Confronted by the best that's been thought and said, he's come to reconsider his values and views. What was once flat dogma turns into lively commitment and conviction.

But I think that the experience of change is at the heart of literary education. How does it come about? For me, it had a long foreground to be sure, but most immediately I was guided by a teacher. He told me that I—I in particular—might get something worth keeping out of *The Autobiography of Malcolm X*. And I suspect that's how many of us teachers found the books that have made us who we are. Teachers who've been inspired by great works have been moved to pass the gift on. "What we have loved, others will love," says Wordsworth, addressing his friend Coleridge in *The Prelude*—"and we will teach them how."

I think that the highest objective for someone trying to provide a literary education to students is to make such moments of transformation possible. Teachers set the scene for secular conversion. These conversions may be large scale—like the one that Whitman seems to have undergone when he read Emerson's "The Poet" and realized that though Emerson could not himself become the American poet prophesied in the essay, he, Walt Whitman, actually could. But the changes that literary art rings can be relatively minor, too. Reading a book may make a person more receptive to beauty than he otherwise would have been; might make him more sensitive to injustice; more prone to be self-reliant. Granted, books can have negative effects, too. One has read *Don Quixote*; one has read *Madame Bovary*. The Don is led astray by reading airy books about chivalry—he becomes a knight (and all too often an absurd one) in a post-chivalric time. Everyone who takes off to become a hero in a trash TV show, a cheap movie, or a shoddy book is a sad descendant of Don Quixote. Emma Bovary's fictive life concentrates the lives of all too many people, men and women both, who have drawn their view of love from wish-fulfilling novels. They expect more out of erotic life than erotic life can generally deliver: They turn their erotic lives into their spiritual lives—and that too often ends in failure and disillusionment.

But a prerequisite for sharing literary art with young people should be the belief that overall, its influence can be salutary; it can aid in growth. No one would teach history, after all, if he believed that all, or most, forms of historical knowledge were destructive deceptions; one would not teach music if one felt, as Plato did, that most of it disrupts the harmony of the soul.

I said that transformation was the highest goal of literary education. The best purpose of all art is to inspire, said Emerson, and that seems right to me. But that does not mean that literary study can't have other beneficial effects. It can help people learn to read more sensitively; help them learn to express themselves; it can teach them more about the world at large. But the proper business of teaching is change—for the teacher (who is herself a work in progress) and (preeminently) for the student.

Nor do I think that everyone who picks up a book must seek the sublime moment of unexpected but inevitable connection. People read for diversion, for relaxation, to inform themselves, to stave off anxiety in airplanes when the flight attendant is out of wine and beer. A book can make a good doorstop and a fine paperweight—there's no end of uses for a book. But if you're going to take a book into a room where the objective is to educate people—education being from the Latin *educere*, meaning "lead out of," and then presumably toward something—then you should consider using the book to help lead those who want to go out from their own lives into another, if only a few steps.

If this is what you want to do, then readings will only get in your way. When you launch, say, a Marxist reading of William Blake, you effectively use Marx as a tool of analysis and judgment. To the degree that Blake anticipates Marx, Blake is prescient and to be praised. Thus the Marxist reading approves of Blake for his hatred of injustice, his polemic against imperialism, his suspicion of the gentry, his critique of bourgeois art as practiced by the likes of Sir Joshua Reynolds. But Blake, being Blake, also diverges from Marx. He is, presumably, too committed to something akin to liberal individualism; he doesn't understand the revolutionary potential latent in the proletariat; he is, perhaps, an idealist who believes that liberation of consciousness matters more than—or at least must precede—material liberation; he has no clear theory of class conflict. Thus Blake, admirable as he may be, needs to be read with skepticism; he requires a corrective, and the name of that corrective is Karl Marx. Just so, the corrective could also be called Jacques Derrida (who would illuminate Blake the logocentrist); Foucault (who would demonstrate Blake's immersion in and implicit endorsement of an imprisoning society); Kristeva (who would be attuned to Blake's imperfections on the score of gender politics); and so on down the line. The current sophisticated critic would be unlikely to pick one master to illuminate the work at hand—he would mix and match as the occasion required. But to enact a reading means to submit one text to the terms of another; to allow one text to interrogate another—then often to try, sentence, and summarily execute it.

The problem with the Marxist reading of Blake is that it robs us of some splendid opportunities. We never take the time to arrive at a Blakean reading of Blake, and we never get to ask whether Blake's vision might be true—by which I mean, following William James, whether it's good in the way of belief. The moment when the student in the classroom or the reader perusing the work can pause and say: "Yes, that's how it is; Blake's got it exactly right," disappears. There's no chance for the instant that Emerson and Longinus evoke, when one feels that he's written what he's only read, uttered what he's only heard.

Nor—it's worth pointing out—does Marx get much real opportunity here either. He's assumed to be a superior figure: There are in fact any number of Marxist readings of Blake out there; I know of no Blakean readings of Marx. But the student who has heard the teacher unfold a Marxist reading of a work probably doesn't get to study Marx per se. He never gets to have a potential moment of revelation reading *The Manifesto* or *The Grundrisse*. Marx too disappears from the scene, becoming part of a technological apparatus for processing other works. No one asks: Is what Marx is saying true? Is Foucault on to something? Is what Derrida believes actually the case? They're simply applied like paint to the side of a barn; the paint can go on roughly or it can go on adroitly, with subtle variations of mood and texture. But paint is what it is.

It should be clear here that my objection isn't to theoretical texts per se. If a fellow professor thinks that Marx or Foucault or Kristeva provides a contribution to the best that has been thought and said, then by all means read and study the text. (I've studied these writers with students and not without profit.) But the teacher who studies, say, Foucault probably needs to ask what kind of life Foucault commends. Is it one outside of all institutions? Is it one that rebels against all authority? Can that life be in any way compatible with life as a professor or a student? These are questions that are rarely asked about what are conceived of as the more radical thinkers of the era. It is not difficult to guess why this is so.

I've said that the teacher's job is to offer a Blakean reading of Blake, or an Eliotic reading of Eliot, and that's a remark that can't help but raise questions. The standard for the kind of interpretation I have in mind is actually rather straightforward. When a teacher admires an author enough to teach his work, then it stands to reason that the teacher's initial objective ought to be framing a reading that the author would approve. The teacher, to begin with, represents the author: He analyzes the text sympathetically, he treats the words with care and caution and with due respect. He works hard with the students to develop a vision of what the world is and how to live that rises from the author's work and that, ultimately, the author, were he present in the room, would endorse. Northrop Frye does something very much like this in his book on Blake, *Fearful Symmetry*; George Orwell achieves something similar in his famous essay on Dickens. In both cases, the critic's objective is to read the author with humane sensitivity, then synthesize a view of life that's based on that reading. Schopenhauer tells us that all major artists ask and in their fashion answer a single commanding question: "What is life?" The critic works to show how the author frames that query and how he answers it. Critics are necessary for this work because the answers that most artists give to major questions are indirect. Artists move forward through intuition and inference: They feel their way to their sense of things. The critic, at his best, makes explicit what is implicit in the work.

This kind of criticism is itself something of an art, not a science. You cannot tell that you have compounded a valid reading of Dickens any more than that you have compounded a valid novel or a valid play. When others find your Dickensian endorsement of Dickens to be of use to them, humanly, intellectually, spiritually, then your endorsement is a success. The desire to turn the art of reading into a science is part of what draws the profession to the application of sterile concepts.

Perhaps an analogy will be helpful. Let us say that a friend of ours has been seriously ill, or gone through a bad divorce, or has fallen wildly, unexpectedly in love. The friend tells us all about it, from beginning to end, with all the sensitivity she can muster. The story is long and complex and laced with nuance. We listen patiently and take it in. Later on we're faced with explaining this situation to a third person, a mutual friend of us both.

Our confiding friend, our first one, wants this to happen: She wants her friends to know the story. How do we proceed? Surely we proceed as sensitively and humanely as possible. We honor our first friend's way of understanding the illness or the love affair. If we are a good friend, we tell the story such that, were the first friend there in the room, she would nod with gratitude.

We may not believe the first friend's entire sense of the story. We may have a different idea of what happened and why. But we honor our first friend by keeping true to her insofar as we can. We do not, say, begin with a Freudian or Marxist reinterpretation of what it is she has told us. If we do, we are no friend at all. We have not given someone we care about due consideration.

Just so, we need to befriend the texts that we choose to teach. They too are the testaments of human beings who have lived and suffered in the world. They too deserve honor and respect. If you have a friend whose every significant utterance you need to translate into another idiom—whose two is not the real two, as Emerson says—then that is a friend you need to jettison. That is simply to say that you do not need to keep company with someone you take to be a liar. If there are texts that you cannot befriend, then leave them to the worms of time—or to the kinder ministrations of others.

In a once famous essay, "Against Interpretation," Susan Sontag denounced interpretation and called for an "erotics of art." She wanted immersion in the text, pleasure, the drowning of self-consciousness. She sought ecstatic immediacy. To be against readings, as I am, is not to be against interpretation. Interpretation entails the work, often difficult, often pleasurable, of parsing the complexities of meaning a given text offers. It means being alert to connotation; it means reading for tone; it means being able to make what is implicit in a piece of writing clearly explicit. Interpretation is necessary if we are to decide what vision of the world the text endorses.

To be against readings is also not to be against criticism. Once the author's vision of what Wallace Stevens calls "how to live, what to do" is made manifest, it's necessary to question it. In time, I learned to ask whether Malcolm X's views about Jews and women were conducive to a good life for anyone. His sense of race relations, early and late in the book, also needed some examination and some skeptical questioning. But this sort of questioning needs to occur once the author's vision is set forth in a comprehensive, clear, sympathetic manner. Criticism is getting into skeptical dialogue with the text. Mounting a conventional academic reading—applying an alternative set of terms—means closing off the dialogue before it has a chance to begin.

You may find that after you've listened to your friend's story about her love affair or divorce that you can't buy everything she says. Her vision is self-idealizing or skewed. Then, as a friend, you need to bring your reservations forward and discuss them with her. So it is with the text: The teacher and students inquire into it, and often too they answer on its behalf. But it all begins with a simple gesture. It all begins by befriending the text.

That gesture of befriending should have a public as well as a classroom dimension. The books that we professors of literature tend now to write are admirable in many ways. They are full of learning, hard work, honesty, and intelligence that sometimes in its way touches on brilliance. But they are also, at least in my judgment, usually unreadable. They are composed as performances. They are meant to show, and often to show off, the prowess of the author. They could not conceivably be meant to provide spiritual or intellectual nourishment. No one could read a representative instance of such writing and decide, based on it, to change her life. Our books are not written from love but from need.

I think that it is possible to write books and essays on behalf of literature that will demonstrate its powers of renovation and inquire into the limits of those powers. Such books can and should be inspiring not only to members of the profession but to educated (or self-educated) and curious members of the general public who are willing to do some hard intellectual work. As a profession, our standing in and impact upon society beyond our classrooms now is minuscule. Yet we are copiously stocked with superb talent: Some of the best young minds in America continue to be drawn to the graduate study of literature. But unless we professors change our ways and stop seeking respectability and institutional standing at the expense of genuine human impact, we are destined, as Tennyson has it, to rust unburnished, never to shine in use.

One must admit that it's possible to develop too exalted a sense of the transforming powers of literature and the other arts. What worked for me and you may not have a universal application. It's probable that most people will be relatively content to live within the ethical and conceptual world that their parents and their society pass on to them. Edmund Burke and Samuel Johnson thought of common-sense opinion as a great repository of wisdom stored through the ages, augmented and revised through experience, trial and error, until it became in time the treasure of humanity. Perhaps the conservative sages were right. But there will always be individuals who cannot live entirely by the standard dispensation and who require something better—or at least something else. This group may be small (though I think it larger than most imagine), but its members need what great writing can bring them very badly indeed. We professors of literature hold the key to the warehouse where the loaves lie fresh and steaming while outside people hunger for them, sometimes dangerously. We ought to do all we can to open the doors and dispense the bread: We should see how far it'll go.

NARCISSUS REGARDS HIS BOOK/
THE COMMON READER NOW

W HO IS THE common reader now? I do not think that there is any way to evade a simple answer to this question. Common readers—which is to say the great majority of people who continue to read—read for one purpose and one purpose only. They read for pleasure. They read to be entertained. They read to be diverted, assuaged, comforted, and tickled.

The evidence for this phenomenon is not far to seek. Check out the best-seller lists, even in the exalted *New York Times*. See what Oprah's reading. Glance at the Amazon top one hundred. Look around on the airplane. The common reader—by which I don't mean the figure evoked by Doctor Johnson and Virginia Woolf, but the person toting a book on the train or loading one into his iPod or Kindle or whatever—the contemporary common reader reads for pleasure, and easy pleasure at that. Reading, where it exists at all, has largely become a relatively unprofitable wing of the diversion industry.

Life in America now is all too often one of two things. Often it is work. People work very hard indeed—often it takes two incomes to support a family, and few are the full-time professional jobs that currently require only forty hours a week. And when life is not work, what is it? When life isn't work, it is play. That's not hard to understand. People are tired, stressed, drained: They want to kick back a little. That something done in the rare off-hours should be strenuous seems rather unfair. Frost talked about making his vocation and his avocation one, and about his work being play for mortal stakes: For that sort of thing, assuming it was ever possible, there is no longer the time.

But it's not only the division of experience between hard labor and empty leisure that now makes reading for something like mortal stakes a very remote possibility. Not all that long ago—fifteen years, not much more—students paraded through the campuses and through the quads, chanting variations on a theme: Hey-hey, ho-ho, they jingled, Western culture's got to go. The marches and the chants and the general skepticism about something called the canon seemed to some an affront to all civilized values.

But maybe not. Maybe this was a moment of real inquiry on the kids' part. What was this thing called Western culture? Who created it? Who sanctioned it? Most important—what was so valuable about it? Why did it matter to study a poem by Blake, or to ponder a Picasso or comprehend the poetry latent in the religions of the world?

I'm not sure that the teachers and scholars ever offered a very good answer to those implied queries. The conservatives, protected by tenure, immersed in the minutiae of their fields, slammed the windows closed and cranked the radiators when the parade passed by. They went on with what they were doing. Those who concurred with the students brought mikes and drums themselves and joined the march. They were much in demand in the media—figures of great interest. The *Post* was calling; the *Times* was on the other line. Was it true? Were the professors actually repudiating the works that they had purportedly been retained to preserve?

It was true—and there was more, the rebels yelled. They thought they would have the microphones in their hands all day and all of the night. They imagined that teaching Milton with an earring in one ear would never cease to fascinate the world.

But it did. The media—most inconstant of lovers—came and the media went, and the academy was left with its cultural authority in tatters. How could it be otherwise? The news outlets sell one thing above all others, and that is not so much the news as it is newness. What one buys when one buys a daily paper, what one purchases when one purchases a magazine, is the hypothesis that what is going on right now is amazing, unprecedented, stunning. Or at least worthy of intense concentration. What has happened in the past is of correspondingly less interest. In fact, it may barely be of any interest at all. Those who represented the claims of the past should never have imagined that the apostles of newness would give them a fair hearing or a fair rendering, either.

Now the people who were kids when the Western canon went on trial and received summary justice are working the levers of culture. They are the editors and the reviewers and the arts feature writers and the ones who interview the novelists and the poets—to the degree that anyone interviews the poets. Though the arts interest them, though they read this and they read that—there is one thing that makes them very nervous indeed about what they do. They are not comfortable with—errrr—judgments of quality. They are not at ease with "the whole evaluation thing." They may sense that Blake's *Songs* are in some manner more valuable, more worth pondering, more worth preserving than *The Simpsons*. They may *sense* as much. But they do not have the terminology to explain why. They never heard the arguments. The professors who should have been providing them when the No More Western Culture marches were going on never made a significant peep. They never quoted Matthew Arnold on the best that's been thought and said—that would have been embarrassing. They never quoted Emerson on the right use of reading—that might have been silly. (It's to inspire.) They never told their students how Wordsworth saved Mill's life by restoring to him his ability to feel. They never showed why difficult pleasure might be superior to easy ones. They never even cited Wilde on the value of pure and simple literary pleasure.

The academy failed and continues to fail to answer the question of value, or to echo the best of the existing answers. But entertainment culture suffers no such difficulty. Its rationale is simple, clear, and potent. The products of the culture industry are good because they make you feel good. They produce immediate and readily perceptible pleasure. Beat that, Alfred, Lord Tennyson. Touch it if you can, Emily Dickinson.

So the arbiters of culture—the academy's former students—went the logical way. They said: If it makes you feel good, it must be. If Stephen King and John Grisham bring pleasure, why, then let us applaud them. Let's give them awards, let's break down the walls of the old clubs and colleges and give them entry forthwith. The only really important question to pose about a novel by Stephen King, we now know, is whether it offers a vintage draught of the Stephen King experience. Does it deliver the spine-shaking chills of great King efforts past? Is the mayhem cranked to the desirable degree? Do homebody sadists and ordinary everyday masochists get what they want and need from the product?

What's not asked in the review and the interview and the profile is whether a King book is worth writing or worth the reading. It seems that no one anymore has the wherewithal to say that reading a King novel is a major waste of human time. No chance. If people want to read it, if they get pleasure from it, then it must be good. What other standard is there?

Media now do not seek to shape taste. They do not try to educate the public. And this is so in part because no one seems to know what literary and cultural education would consist of. What does make a book great anyway? And public media do not try to shape taste for another reason: It annoys the readers. They feel insulted, condescended to—they feel dumb. And no one, now, will pay you for making him feel dumb. Public entertainment generally works in just the opposite way—by making the consumer feel like a genius. No, even the most august publications and broadcasts no longer attempt to shape taste. They merely seek to reflect it. They hold the cultural mirror up to the reader—what the reader likes, the writer and the editor like. They hold the mirror up to the reader and—what else can he do?—the reader falls in love. The common reader today is someone who has fallen in love—with himself.

Freud tells us that people tend to love after two patterns— we are narcissistic lovers or we are anaclitic lovers. We either love versions of ourselves or we love others based on idealized imagoes from childhood. What Freud does not say, but may be true nonetheless, is that a culture can draw people away from anaclitic or idealizing love in the direction of love of self. Our culture, which revolves around the imperial prerogatives and consumer pleasures of self, seems to have done precisely that.

Narcissus in his current post-Freudian guise looks into the book review and finds it good. Narcissus peers into Amazon's top one hundred, and lo, he feels the love. Nothing insults him; nothing pulls him away from that gorgeous smooth watery image below. The editor sells it to him cheap; the professor who might want to intervene—coming on like that Miltonic voice does to Eve gazing lovingly on herself in the pool: "What thou seest / What there thou seest . . . is thyself," it says—the professor has other things to do.

The intervening voice in Milton (and in Ovid, Milton's original in this) is a source of influence. Is it possible that in the world now there are people who might suffer not from an anxiety that they might be influenced but rather from an anxiety that they might never be? Perhaps not everyone loves himself with complete conviction and full abandon. Maybe there remain those who look into the shimmering flattering glass of current culture and do not quite like what they see. Maybe life isn't working for them as well as it is supposed to for all in this immeasurably rich and unprecedentedly free country.

Reading in pursuit of influence—that I think is the desired thing. It takes a strange mixture of humility and confidence to do as much. For suppose one reads anxious about *not being influenced*. To do so is to admit that one is imperfect, searching, unfinished. It's difficult to do when one is young, at least at present: Some of the oldest individuals I meet lately are under the age of twenty-one. It is difficult to do when one is in middle age: for that is the time of commitments. One has a husband or a wife, a family and job, and—who knows?—a career. Having second thoughts then looks like a form of weakness: It makes everyone around you insecure. One must stand steady and sometimes one must pretend. And in old age—early or late—how can one still be a work in progress? That's the time, surely, to have assumed one's permanent form. That's the time to have balanced accounts, gained traction, become the proper statue to commemorate one's proper life.

Of his attempts at works of art, one writer observed: Finished? They are never finished. At a certain point someone comes and takes them away. (At a certain point, something comes and takes us away—where, we do not know.) We too are never truly finished. What Narcissus wanted was completion, wholeness: He wanted to *be* that image in the water and have done with it. There would be no more time, no more change, no more revision. To be willing to be influenced, even up to the last, is tantamount to declaring that we'll never be perfect, never see as gods see—even that we don't know who and what we are, why (if for any reason) we are here, and where we'll go.

The desire to be influenced is always bound up with some measure of self-dislike, or at least with a dose of discontent. While the current culture tells us to love ourselves as we are—or as we will be after we've acquired the proper products and services— the true common reader does not find himself adequate at all. He looks in the mirror of his own consciousness and he is anything but pleased. *That* is not what he had in mind at all. That is not what *she* was dreaming of.

But where is this common reader—this impossible, possible man or woman who is both confident and humble, both ready to change and skeptical of all easy remedies? *That* common reader is in our classrooms, in our offices, before the pages of our prose and poems, watching and wondering and hoping to be brought, by our best ministrations and our love, into being.

THE UNCOOLNESS OF
GOOD TEACHERS

THERE'S A SCENE in the movie *Almost Famous* that, at least for my money, can tell you as much about good teaching as a term's worth of courses at any currently flourishing graduate school of education. William Miller, aspiring rock journalist, is talking on the phone to the old pro, Lester Bangs. William's working on a profile of a group called Stillwater (whose music doesn't run terribly deep), and some of the band members have been softening him up—making friends with him. Don't buy it, says Bangs. "They make you feel cool. And hey. I met you. You are not cool." William has to confess as much: "Even when I thought I was," he says, "I knew I wasn't." But then Lester Bangs opens up, too: "*We're* uncool," he proclaims. And though uncool people don't tend to get the girl, being uncool can help you develop a little spine. It's too easy out there for the handsome and the hip—their work almost never lasts. Then Bangs throws out his rock-Bogart clincher: "The only true currency in this bankrupt world is what we share with someone else when we're uncool."

Bangs is filling the role of teacher here, and he's a pretty good one in large part because he's willing to be uncool and admit it. Why are good teachers strange, uncool, offbeat?

Because really good teaching is about not seeing the world the way that everyone else does. Teaching is about being what people are now prone to call counterintuitive, but to the teacher means simply being honest. The historian sees the election not through the latest news blast but in the context of presidential politics from Washington to the present. The biologist sees a natural world that's not calmly picturesque but a jostling, striving, evolving contest of creatures in quest of reproduction and survival. The literature professor won't accept the current run of standard, hip clichés but demands bursting metaphors and ironies of an insinuatingly serpentine sort. The philosopher wants an argument as escape-proof as an iron box: What currently passes for logic makes him want to grasp himself by the hair and yank himself out of his seat.

Good teachers perceive the world in alternative ways and they strive to get their students to test out these new, potentially enriching perspectives. Sometimes they do so in ways that are, to say the least, peculiar. The philosophy prof steps in through the window the first day of class and asks her students to write down the definition of the world *door.* The elementary school teacher sees that his kids can't figure out how the solar system works by looking at the astronomy book. So he takes them outside and designates each one as a planet or a major moon and gets them rotating *and* revolving around each other in the grassy field. (For his own safety—and perhaps for other reasons—he plays the part of the sun.) The high school teacher, struck by his kids' conformity, performs an experiment. He sends the hippest guy in the class off on an errand, and while he's gone draws pairs of lines on the board, some equal, some unequal. When the hip kid comes back, he asks the class, who're in on the game, which lines are the same length, which are different, and, as they've been instructed, they answer the wrong way. They're surprised at how often the cool kid disobeys the evidence of his own eyes and goes along with the pack; a few hours later, at home, they're surprised at how good they were at fooling their friend, and how much pleasure they took in making him the butt of the experiment.

From the standard vantage point, these gambits can look like pointlessly offbeat things to do. But the good teacher knows that they can crack the shell of convention and help people look freshly at life. The good teacher is sometimes willing to be a little ridiculous: He wears red or green socks so a kid will always have an excuse to start a conversation with him; she bumbles with her purse to make her more maladroit kids feel at ease.

Good teachers know that now, in what's called the civilized world, the great enemy of knowledge isn't ignorance, though ignorance will do in a pinch. The great enemy of knowledge is knowingness. It's the feeling encouraged by TV and movies and the Internet that you're on top of things and in charge. You're hip and always know what's up. Good teachers are constantly fighting against knowingness by asking questions, creating difficulties, raising perplexities. And they're constantly dramatizing their own aversion to knowingness in the way they walk and talk and dress—in their willingness to go the Lester Bangs route.

Needless to say, teachers can get a lot out of unorthodox teaching, too. The person who turned the bunch of elementary school kids into a spinning solar system wasn't a freshly minted Master of Arts in Teaching. It was Ludwig Wittgenstein, the most influential Western philosopher of the twentieth century. Wittgenstein spent time at Cambridge, arguing with Bertrand Russell and terrorizing undergraduates, but he also did stints as an elementary school teacher. He seems to have loved these gigs and to have been good at them, though he was prone to pull the ears of students slow to master their math facts. Wittgenstein probably found that by getting out of the conventional high-powered university he could let his thoughts loose, ponder things in a freer and less constrained way. After the elementary school teaching run, Wittgenstein went to work on what would become *Philosophical Investigations*, as original a piece of philosophy as the twentieth century produced. In it, he was not unwilling to get down to basics. The former grade school teacher wasn't afraid to pose elementary questions.

But a lot of teachers want to be with it. Unlike Lester (and Ludwig), many of them, maybe even most, want to be cool. How do you become a hip teacher? It's pretty easy, actually. You emulate your students. You do what they do, but with a little bit of adult élan. You like what they like: listen to their tunes, immerse in their technology. In this way, you can get popular fast, but you're also letting the students become *your* teachers.

The most common way to become a hip teacher now—there have been other ways; there will be more—is to go wild for computers. Students love computers; you get points for loving them more. At my school a prof whose energy and ingenuity I have to admire provides his students with handheld wireless input gizmos that have a dozen buttons on them. (I understand they look like TV remotes—not a good sign.) Every five or ten minutes, the prof stops teaching and checks with the kids to see if they're following along. Cool. Many other teachers have turned their classes into light and laser shows. Around the corner, we can expect 3-D glasses.

In order to stay current and be hip, teachers have let students bring their computers into the classroom. There, behind the screens, they do many things, which may include taking class notes or looking up references the teacher makes. But then, too, they may not. Many current teachers are afraid to ban computers from their classrooms. It'll make them unpopular, unhip.

Anyone tempted by this mode of going about things, where the teacher and the student switch roles, should consider the philosophy of education put forward by a chaired senior colleague of Lester Bangs, someone who achieved yet greater distinction as an on-screen pedagogue and who provides one of the constant refrains of this book. "Whatever it is," Groucho Marx merrily sang in *Horse Feathers*, "I'm against it." If it's TV and cultural studies, I'm against it; if it's computers and the hype that surrounds the wireless classroom, I'm against it.

A good teacher is often a Groucho Marxist because the job is to provide alternatives to *whatever* is out there. It's to provide an alternative to convention and conformity. Convention fits some people, but not all. (Maybe not even most.) In fact, even the most conventionally minded people often relish putting aside their conformity for a while and exposing their hidden sides. And here the genius of Lester Bangs–style pedagogy really shines through. "The only true currency in this bankrupt world," he says, "is what we share with someone else *when* we're uncool." When. Uncoolness can be a state that anyone slides into, a state where we're more open, vulnerable, and susceptible to being surprised than at other times when we've got the cold deflective armor on. Teachers live for the moments when their students—and they themselves—cast off the breastplates and iron masks and open up. And good teachers are always ready for those moments to happen.

"I'm glad you were home," William tells Bangs after they've had their rock heart-to-heart on the telephone.

"I'm always home," Bangs assures him. "I'm uncool."

TEACHING THE TRUTHS

STANDING IN FRONT of me is the World Spirit, the zeit-geist, the Rude Beast Slouching Towards Bethlehem, or at least he's a significant contender for the role. But the odd thing is that the Spirit, who is decked in thick glasses, weary heel-worn shoes, and an affectionately tended goatee, is refusing to act the part. Before *him* is a lot of the sort of detritus that ought to be swept into the dustbin of history—me, that is, and a hand-ful of other humanities professors—and he has a right, it would seem, to scoff at us human irrelevancies once or twice, then flourish the broom. But that's not what he's doing. The Spirit of the Age talks a lot, almost uncontrollably, about his great love, computers, and he flies off occasionally into hyperlinked digressions, mentally double clicking on phrases from off-the-point sentences past, but by and large the Spirit seems a pretty nice guy.

We're here, we half a dozen or so professors, to learn how to "integrate computing into humanities instruction." In return for sitting through a few training sessions and promising to use technology in a course sometime, we each get temporary use of a jazzy laptop computer. Integrating computing into humanities instruction: This is code, really, for transferring as much as possible of what we know and can do over to the computer. I'm learning how to set up websites full of information about the courses I'm teaching. At the website for my class on dystopias and utopias, Beyond *1984*, you should be able to access all the reading, the relevant articles, my notes for lectures and presentations, your classmates' essays. In the chat room I could set up, you'd talk on with your fellow dys- and utopic students. If I arrange things right, another university computer advocate has informed me, my workload will sink "exponentially."

"Exponentially." Hmmm. In fact, as I figure it, the workload will near the vanishing point. I'll only be needed to grade the papers. I won't be gone, per se; tenure will probably protect me, no matter how flagrantly irrelevant I become. No, I'm heading to the metaphorical dustbin, but my graduate students may be going there literally. We humanities professors are, it would seem, over, played out. The World Spirit doesn't need to gloat; he can just pass serenely through, like the whirlwind angel in Exodus, blowing the husks and shells into the desert and away.

The Exodus angel may be on to something. We humanities professors *have* been working to put ourselves beside the point. (Though maybe it's not too late . . .) So there's no reason why, if things continue in their current course, the cheerful logorrheic in front of me won't have his way.

One example: The teaching of writing has been all but transformed over the past decade. Many teachers once regarded writing as a way to unfold and even to discover an inner self. Writing was, to take a phrase from Keats, a form of "Soul-making." A flexible, potent individual style signified supple, developing character. Now we know better. Writing, it turns out, is a technology. It's a way of transferring information from one site to another. Thus it needs to be clean, clear, fluent, but also rather anonymous, unclouded by excess metaphor or perplexing irony. One learns "communication," not self-excavation, self-making.

Now that the computer is at the center of every course, every area of inquiry is more and more defined by the resources of the computer. Computers are splendid research tools. Good: More and more the curriculum turns in the direction of research. We don't attempt to write as Dickens would, to experiment with thinking as he might, were he alive today. Rather, we research Dickens. We delve into his historical context, learn what the newspapers were gossiping about on the day installment one of *Bleak House* hit the stands. We shape our tools, as Marshall McLuhan famously said, and thereafter our tools shape us.

One can be fully grateful for the best blessings of technology. One can be receptive to many of the pleasures that come out of American popular culture. Yet one can still feel, as I do, that education needs to be about more than training and entertaining, about learning how to do a lucrative job and how to disperse the money that job creates. William Carlos Williams said that people die every day for want of what's to be found in "despised poems." Hyperbolical as the line may be, I think there's something to it. We need the study of history and literature and art, and as more than modes of diversion and more than testing grounds for practical skills.

But what is it precisely that the humanities offer? Pragmatically, what can they do?

The answers I'll offer are both old and new, both conservative and radical, geared to bring full comfort to neither left nor right. And the answers begin where good taste demands that, as of now, one shouldn't tread.

I teach at the University of Virginia, and not far from me down Route 29, in Lynchburg, Virginia, is the church of Jerry Falwell. Falwell, it's well-known, taught the word of God, the literal, unarguable truth as it was revealed to him in the Bible, and as it must be understood by all heaven-bound Christians.

For some time, I thought that we at the University of Virginia had nothing consequential to do with the Reverend Falwell. Occasionally, I get a book through interlibrary loan from Falwell's Liberty University; sometimes the inside cover contains a warning to the pious suggesting that though this volume may be the property of the Liberty University library, its contents, insofar as they contradict the Bible (which means the Bible according to Falwell), are of no particular value.

It's said that when a certain caliph was on the verge of burning the great library at Alexandria, scholars fell on their knees in front of him and begged him to reconsider. "There are two kinds of books here," the caliph reputedly said. "There are those that contradict the Koran—they are blasphemous. And there are those that corroborate the Koran—they are superfluous." And then: "Burn the library." Given the possibilities that the caliph's behavior opened up, it's a good thing that Liberty has a library at all.

Thomas Jefferson, our founder, was a deist (maybe worse than that, the orthodox of Virginia used to whisper). The architecture of the university's central grounds, designed by Jefferson, is emphatically pre-Christian, based on Greek and Roman models. In fact the Rotunda, once the university's library, is designed in homage to the Roman Pantheon, a temple to the twelve chief pagan gods. As soon as they saw the university, local divines became apoplectic. Where was the church? Unlike Princeton and Harvard, the university didn't have a Christian house of worship in its midst. From pulpits all over Virginia, ministers threatened the pagan enclave with ruin from above.

Jefferson—deist (maybe worse), scientist, revolutionary, seems to have believed that the best way to deal with religion was to banish it, formally, from the university, then go on to teach the useful arts of medicine, commerce, law, and the rest. The design of my university declares victory over what the radicals of the Enlightenment would have called superstition, and what most Americans currently call faith or spirituality. And we honor Jefferson now by, in effect, rendering unto Falwell that which is Falwell's.

In fact, humanists in general have entered into an implied bargain with Falwell & Company. They do the soul crafting. They administer the spiritual education. They address the hearts of the students—and in some measure of the nation at large. We preside over the minds. We shape intelligences; we train the faculties. In other words, we teachers cut an implicit deal with religion and its promulgators. They do their thing, we do ours. But isn't that the way it should be? Isn't religion private? Spirituality, after all, is everyone's personal affair. It shouldn't be at the core of college education; it should be passed over in silence. What professor would have the bad taste to puncture the walls of his students' privacy by asking them uncomfortable questions about ultimate values?

Well, me. But then, I got into the teaching business for the reason, I suspect, that many people did. I thought it was a high-stakes affair, a place where, for want of a better way to put it, souls are won and lost. I thought Socrates' line about summed it up: "This discussion," he said, referring to an exchange with his students, "is not about any chance question, but about the way that one ought to lead one's life."

"How do you imagine God?" If you're going to indulge in embarrassing behavior, if you're going to make your students "uncomfortable" (still often the worst thing for a student to be now), why not go all the way? This, or some variant, is the question that lately has been inaugurating my classes—not classes in religion but classes in Shakespeare, in Romantic poetry, in major nineteenth-century novels. That is, the embarrassing question begins courses of study with which—according to Jefferson, according to Falwell, according to the great majority of my colleagues in the humanities—such a query has nothing to do.

What kind of answers do I get? Quite marvelous ones, often. After the students who are disposed to walk out have, sometimes leaving an editorial sigh hanging in the air, and there's been time for reflection and some provisional writing, answers come. Here I can provide only a taste of them.

Some of the accounts are on the fluffy side. I've learned, or relearned, the view that God is love and only love; I've heard that God is nature, that God is light, that God is all the goodness in the universe. I hear tales about God's interventions into the lives of my students, interventions that save them from accidents and deliver them from sickness while others fall by the way. There's a whole set of accounts that are on the all-benevolent side—smiling, kindly, but more than a little under-ramified, insufficiently thought-out. If God is all things, or abides in all things, as I've heard it said, what is the source of evil? (By now it's clear to the students that bad taste is my métier—once this is understood, they can be quite indulgent.) A pause, then often an answer, sometimes not a bad one. The most memorable of the exponents of smiling faith was a woman named Susan who called her blend of creamy benevolence—what else?—Susanism.

Some of the responses are anything but under-elaborated. These tend to come from orthodoxly religious students, many of whom are well trained, maybe overtrained, in the finer points of doctrine. I get some hard-core believers. But it would be difficult to call them Falwell's children, because they're often among the most thoughtful students in the class. They, unlike the proponents of the idea that God is light, period, are interested in major questions. They care about knowing the source of evil. They want to know what it means to live a good life. And though they're rammed with doctrine, they're not always creatures of dogma. There's often more than a little room for doubt. And even if their views are sometimes rock-wall solid, these students don't mind being tested. They're willing to put themselves into play because, given their interests, they don't mind that this "is not about any chance question, but about the way that one ought to lead one's life."

Religion is a good place to start a humanities course, even if what we're going on to do is read the novels of Henry James, in part because religion is likely to be the place where you can find what the philosopher (and anti-philosopher) Richard Rorty calls a person's "final vocabulary." A final vocabulary is the ultimate set of terms that we use in order to confer value on experience. It's where our principles lie. When someone talks about the Ten Commandments, or the Buddha's four noble truths, or the innate goodness of human beings in their natural state, or history being the history of class conflict, and does so with a passion, then in all likelihood the person has revealed the core of her being. She's touched on her ultimate terms of commitment, the point beyond which mere analysis cannot go. Rorty puts it this way: "All human beings carry about a set of words which they employ to justify their actions, their beliefs, and their lives. These are the words in which we formulate praise of our friends and contempt of our enemies, our long-term projects, our deepest self-doubts and our highest hopes. They are the words in which we tell, sometimes prospectively and sometimes retrospectively, the story of our lives."

Sometimes there's apparently no "there" there. That is, the students seem to have no ultimate vocabularies. The anti-philosophy of "whatever" is in place. But that can be a merely superficial condition. If you keep asking, values often do emerge. And when they don't, the students sometimes are willing to ask themselves why. Somehow they feel the pain of that void. They feel what Kundera, thinking of Nietzsche, called an unbearable lightness of being. Within that void, or against the solid wall of conviction, humanistic learning can fruitfully take place.

In Rorty's idiom, the word "final" is ironic. That is, a major step in educating oneself comes with the conviction that all of one's most dearly held beliefs should be open to change. One's final vocabulary is final only for now. Certain people, says Rorty, "are always aware that the terms in which they describe themselves are subject to change, always aware of the contingency and fragility of their final vocabularies, and thus of their selves." Rorty believes that such people are the exception, not the rule. I'm not so sure. I think that one can begin by assuming that any student who turns up in a humanities course is open to influence, open to change.

It's time, perhaps, for something like a thesis statement: The function of a liberal arts education, as I see it, is to rejuvenate, reaffirm, replenish, revise, overwhelm, replace, reorder, or maybe just slightly retouch the web of words that Rorty calls the final vocabulary. A language, Wittgenstein thought, is a way of life. A new language, whether we learn it from a historian, a poet, a painter, or a composer of music, is potentially also a new way to live.

While I'm asking my questions about imagining God, what's going on in the classrooms of colleagues down the hall and across the country?

Often some very good things. (It's not all training, not all entertaining.) No matter what humanities teachers may profess in their published papers, in the classrooms matters are often much different. Professors of literature and history and philosophy and religious studies generally have something in common. They attempt to teach one essential power, and they often do so with marked success. That one thing is reading. They cultivate attentiveness to written works, careful consideration, thoughtful balancing, coaxing out of disparate meanings, responsiveness to the complexities of sense. They try—we try, for I'm of this party, too—to help students become more and more like what Henry James said every author should be, someone on whom nothing is lost. Attentiveness to words and, with the habits of concentration developed on words, an attentiveness to life—that is one aim of a humanities education.

But there are limits to close reading. It's said that the Harvard scholar Walter Jackson Bate used to do a Marx Brothers–style routine to dramatize them. "Close reading," he'd mutter, and push the book up near his nose. "Closer reading"—chuckling, digging his face down into the book. Then, finally, "very close reading," where nose and book kissed and not a word of print was legible. The point is that with a certain kind of exclusive attention to the page, life disappears. The connection between word and world goes dark.

This is the fate of reading when we do not move beyond interpretation. It is possible, I fully believe, to read a book in such a way that we can bring forth an interpretation that the author would approve. We can, with careful study, with disciplined effort, concoct a vision of Wordsworth's Nature that the poet would find acceptable; we can imagine what Shelley meant by liberty. We can evoke uncertainties, mysteries, and doubts when those are a poet's Keatsian designs. Critics who do not believe that this is possible may forget how often in day-to-day life we're called upon to relay the story of a protracted illness, a divorce, a long-worked-for triumph as we've heard it recounted by another. Are poems so much more difficult to render?

But then comes the next step, the critical one. I've asked my students what they believe. I've asked them what the word at hand means. Now the final question: Is the work true? That's a question simple to phrase but hard to answer.

Does the work contain live options? Does it offer paths they might wish to take, modes of seeing and saying and doing that they can put into action in the world? How, to phrase the matter in slightly different terms, does the vision at hand, the author's vision, cohere with or combat (or elaborate, or reorder, or simply fail to touch—the possibilities are endless) your own vision of experience, your own final vocabulary?

Do you want to affirm Wordsworth's natural religion? It's not as far-fetched a question as it might sound at a moment when many consider ecological issues to be the ultimate issues on the world's horizon. Is it true what Wordsworth suggests in "Tintern Abbey" about the healing powers of Nature and memory? Can they fight off depression? Not an empty question in an age when antidepressive drugs have become so sadly common. Is Milton's Satan the shape that evil now most often takes—flamboyant, grand, and self-regarding? Or is Blake's Satan—a supreme administrator, mild, bureaucratic, efficient, and congenial, an early exemplar of Hannah Arendt's "banality of evil"—a better emblem? Or, to strike to the center of the tensions that often exist between secular and religious writing, who is the better guide to life, the Jesus of the Gospels or the Prometheus of Percy Bysshe Shelley, who learned so much from Christ but rejected so much as well—in particular Jesus' life of committed celibacy?

Yes, one might say, but those are Romantic writers, polemicists, authors with a program. How about other writers? How about, for instance, the famous poet of negative capability, who seems to affirm nothing, Shakespeare? The most accomplished academic scholars of Shakespeare generally concur: They cannot tell for certain what Shakespeare believed on *any* consequential issue.

But in fact Shakespeare has been the object for what may be the most formidable act of literary criticism yet performed. If Sigmund Freud drew on any author for his vision of human nature—right or wrong as that vision may be—it was Shakespeare. The Oedipal complex, to cite just one of Freud's Shakespearean extractions, ought just as well to be called the Hamlet complex. From Shakespeare, Freud might also have drawn his theories of sibling rivalry; of the tragic antipathy between civilization and the drives; of bisexuality; of patriarchal presumption; of male jealousy; of the intertwinings of love and authority; of humor as an assault on the superego—of a dozen matters more. In larger-scale terms, Freud's tragic sense—his commitment to stoical renunciation as the best response to life's inevitable grief—finds considerable corroboration in the world of Shakespeare's plays. Shakespeare may not have affirmed any ideas directly; he is not, it's true, a polemicist in the way that Blake is. But Freud's contestable truths can be fairly extracted from Shakespeare, put on display, and offered to the judgment of the world. (Rather implicitly and quite brilliantly, Freud succeeds in befriending the spirit of Shakespeare's work in the way that I described in the chapter against readings.) Does Shakespeare/ Freud work? Does their collaboration, if it is fair to call it that, illuminate experience, put one in a profitable relation to life? Does it help you live rightly and enjoy your being in the world?

But what does all of this have to do with religion? Why ask, on day one, the grating question about God?

Because in a fundamental sense Matthew Arnold's view on the relations between poetry and faith is, I believe, an accurate one. If religious faith wanes in the world—or in a given individual—then the next likely source of meaning may well be literature. The literature we have come to value, most especially the novel, is by and large anti-transcendental. It does not offer a vision of the world as existing under the guidance of a deity. It suggests, though often it does not assert, that we humans have to make our own way without the strains and the comforts of faith.

The teaching of literature I want to commend does not argue that always and for everyone a secular, imaginative vision must replace faith. Rather, this sort of teaching says that a most pressing spiritual and intellectual task of the moment is to create a dialogue between religious and secular approaches to life. Many of my students leave class with their religious convictions deepened. They are more ardent and thoughtful believers than when they began. The aim is not conversion. It is the encounter between the transcendental and the worldly. The objective is to help the students place their ultimate narratives in the foreground and render them susceptible to influence.

Most professors of the humanities seem to have little interest in religion as a field of live options. Most of them, from what I can see, have had their crises of faith early in life and have adopted, almost as second nature, a secular view of experience. Others keep their religious commitment separate from their pedagogy and have been doing so for so long that they are hardly aware of it.

But what is old to the teacher is new to the student. The issue of belief matters greatly to the young, or at least it does in my experience. They want to know how to navigate life, what to be, what to do. Matters of faith or worldliness are of great import to our students, and by turning away from them, by continuing our treaty with Falwell where we tutor the mind and he takes the heart and spirit, we do them injustice.

Is it a form of therapy that I am endorsing here? Yes and no. Yes, in that this form of teaching, like Socrates', like Freud's, offers possibilities for change that are not only intellectual but emotional as well. When we're talking about ultimate values, feelings come into play; tensions similar to those met with in a Freudian therapeutic exchange can arise. But there is also a crucial difference. Patients come to psychoanalysis because they suffer from the past—their experience of various events prevents their living with a reasonable fullness in the present. The form of pedagogy I am describing, which is anything but new, assumes a certain ability to live within the present (that is to say, a certain sanity) and so aims itself directly at the future. What *will* you be? What *will* you do?

There is a story about a psychoanalyst who, at the end of the first-day intake interview, asked his patients an unexpected question. "If you were cured, what would you do?" There would come forth a list. "I'd get married." "I'd travel." "I'd come back and study law." To which the therapist sometimes replied, "Well, then, why don't you simply go out and do those things?" At the moment when he posed the possibility, the therapist stopped being a therapist in the Freudian sense and became something rather different.

A scene of instruction can illustrate the kind of teaching I want to commend. One of my recent students, a young woman, professes herself to be an ardent Christian. She believes in doing unto others as you would have them do unto you, in turning the other cheek. She believes Jesus to be the most perfect being. But she reads *The Iliad* and, after a period of languor, she's galvanized by it. What sweeps her in is the vision of a life where triumph matters over everything. The warriors in the poem seek first place all the time. Envy is not a vice to them; it's entirely creditable. The young woman who, it comes out, wants to be a well-to-do corporate lawyer has no trouble seeing something of herself in the unapologetic ambitions of Homer's heroes.

But then, too, she wants to be a Christian. Jesus' originality lies in part in his attempt to supersede the ambition and self-vaunting of Homer's heroes—qualities still very much alive in the Roman empire into which Jesus was born. Which will it be, my student needs to ask herself, Jesus or Achilles? Of course, what she needs is some live synthesis of the two. And it is her task to arrive at it. But without the encounter with Homer, and without our raising the simple and supposedly elementary question of identification—is there anything in you that is Achillean?—she might not have had access to her own divided state. This was an instance not only of reading and interpreting a book—we spent a long time coming to understand the heroic code and considering Homer's highly equivocal attitude toward it—but of allowing the book to interpret and read the reader. It was a moment, I would say, of genuine humanistic education.

The questions I want to ask may seem elementary compared to the sophisticated queries that a theoretically charged Foucauldian may offer in class. But many of us—teachers and students both—do not know what we think about major personal issues. And it is with them that we need to begin. Being a beginner in humanistic inquiry is something to be treasured; sophistication too rapidly attained can be self-defeating. Thus that great violinist on hearing a young, technically brilliant prospective student: "I will never be able to teach him anything. He lacks inexperience." Or Emerson, in a lovely moment from his journals: "Don't let them eat their seed-corn; don't let them anticipate, ante-date, and be young men, before they have finished their boyhood."

What is the teacher's role in this? I think it begins with a realization of what literature and art, at least since the Romantic period, have offered to us. This is the view that there are simply too many sorts of human beings, too many idiosyncratic constitutions, for any simple map of human nature, or any single guide to the good life, to be adaptable for us all. This realization, which coincides with the foundations of widespread democracy as well as with the flourishing of novels, holds that there are multiple ways of apprehending experience and multiple modes of internal organization, or disorder. Accordingly, there are many, many different ways to lead a satisfying, socially constructive life. This, or something like it, is what Milan Kundera is getting at when he calls the characters—and by implication the narrating voices—encountered in fiction "experimental selves." There are multiple ways to go, and confining theories of the self, even those as admirably worked out as, say, Plato's or Kant's, cannot encompass the range of human difference.

The teacher, in other words, begins the secular dialogue with faith by offering the hypothesis that there is no human truth about the good life, but that there are many human truths, many viable paths. To set his students on them, he offers them multiple examples of what Arnold (in what is justifiably the most famous phrase about the objectives of literary education) called the best that has been known and thought. This multiplying of possibilities—a condition enhanced by the rapid diffusion of culture around the globe—makes literature, which is inevitably the effusion of an individual mind, the most likely starting place. I would even say it's the center of humanistic education. As literary works are multiple, so are the number of possibly usable human visions of experience.

Beginning with this hypothesis, the teacher's task is often one of inspired impersonation. Against her students' final vocabularies, against their various faiths, she, with a combination of disinterest and passion, hurls alternatives. Impersonation: The teacher's objective, in the approach I'm describing, is to offer an inspiring version of what is most vital in the author. She merges with the author, becomes the creator, and in doing so makes the past available to the uses of the present. The teacher listens to criticisms, perhaps engenders some herself, but always finally is the author's advocate, his attorney for explication and defense.

Is *The Iliad* a book replete with vital possibilities, or is it a mere historical curiosity? Is it locked in the past, or a potent guide to the present and the future? A number of my students— men and women both—initially thought it was a period piece and nothing more. The way the poem treated women disgusted them. In *The Iliad*, they said, a woman has the status of a few bullocks or a bronze tripod or two. Some, like Helen, are beautiful, and that beauty is a sort of power, but it is a limited and debased one compared to what the men have.

The class was about ready to concur when one of the women students, usually quiet, spoke up. She said that the poem mattered to her because she could see things from Achilles' point of view. The passage that caught her attention first was the one where Achilles' father tells him that he must be the best in every undertaking. He must simply never take second place. "I'm an athlete, I swim," she said, "and that's how I was raised by my parents and my coaches. After a while, though, I had to stop living like that. It's too much."

"Have you ever wanted to go back to it?" someone asked, perhaps me.

"Yes," she said, "all the time. It makes life incredibly intense." And you could see, if you looked hard, that what had once been closed off and left behind began to open again. The life of full unbridled competition is not for everyone, and it will not be approved by all. But if it is your highest aspiration, the thing you most want, then whether you take the path or not, it is worth knowing about your attraction to it. Achilles' life is the life of *thymos*, and if you are, at whatever depths, an individual driven by *thymos*—by the desire for glory and praise, despite the moral censors you've thrown up against that drive—you need to deal with the fact in one way or another. I know no better means to begin to do so than through Homer.

Every essay on education needs a villain. There has to be someone or something preventing the liberal arts from being the world-changing enterprise we all suspect that they can be. And I suppose so far I have supplied a few. There are the spirits of training and of entertaining, and there's the refusal on the part of professors, even the best intentioned, to engage with questions of belief—to hear, in other words, a famous line of Wallace Stevens's: "Say that final belief / Must be in a fiction. It is time to choose." But of course to be a humanist—and the questions that emanate from humanism are ultimately the ones that this essay endorses—one must declare war on what's been called the cultural left, who are supposedly busy condemning all of Western literature for not living up to their own high political standards.

And in one measure, I'm willing to do that. The kind of teaching I part company with, the kind that seems to me most destructive to the freedom of self-making, is the kind that simply applies a standing set of terms to every text that comes to hand. These forms of teaching are a little like bad translation. Every work, alas, is rewritten in the terms of Foucault, of feminism, of Marx, and that is the end of the story.

Surely there are plenty of good questions about gender to pose to *The Iliad*. But if we simply look for a way to apply the theory, apply the denunciation, and do no more, then the free space that helped one student see her own attraction to the athlete's life and helped another to see her divided mind, her pull toward the goodness of the Gospels and the potency that Homer describes—that free space collapses.

And as I have suggested, the theorist almost never turns and interrogates the theoretical terms at hand. He never asks how well Foucault could work as a guide to life. (That is, does he tell a truth?) The theorist generally does not pause to wonder how one would live, if one could live, with the wild hatred of all authority that Foucault endorses. Could you really teach in an institution as authority-based as a university and preach the gospel according to Foucault? It seems to me highly unlikely. But for many theorists, the application of the terms is enough. Rather than sending one nineteenth-century novel after another grinding through the mills of Foucault, why not teach Foucault straight out, and see how much of his purported wisdom can really stand the test of experience? (For myself, I find it hard to think of Foucault without thinking of Emerson's marvelous line: "I hate the builders of dungeons in the air.")

And yet there is a good deal to learn from the cultural left. For, to put it bluntly, they are the ones who believe that books can change people. They don't stop at mere interpretation. They understand that what is at issue in a literary education is belief. In some measure, they've kept the spirit of Socrates alive.

The fall of the liberal arts—which seems to many to be impending—isn't so much about heroes and villains as it is about well-intentioned people forgetting to ask and answer the kinds of questions that got them interested in reading to begin with. Professors, when young, read books as if their lives depended on it; older now, they enjoin their students to read and think as though what chiefly depends on it is their careers.

The spirit of education I want to encourage is better enacted and expressed by Harold Bloom. "We all of us go home each evening and at some moment in time, with whatever degree of overt consciousness, we go over all the signs that the day presented to us. In those signs we seek only what can aid the continuity of our own discourse, the survival of those ongoing qualities that will give what is vital in us even more life. This seeking is the Vichian and the Emersonian making of significance into meaning, by the single test of aiding our survival." This is what we do, or ought to do, with books: turn their signification into meaning, into possibility. So Emerson himself suggests when, asking what the purpose of books is, he says simply that they should contribute to the thing in life that matters most to him. Books should inspire.

And the test of a book, from this perspective, lies in its power to map or transform a life. The question we would ultimately ask of any work of art is this: Can you live it? It you cannot, it may still command considerable interest. The work may charm, it may divert. It may teach us something about the large world; it may convey or refine a remote point. But if it cannot help some of us to imagine a life, or unfold one already latent in us, then it is not a major work, and probably not worth the time of students who, at their period in life, are looking to respond to very pressing questions. They are on the verge of choosing careers, of marrying, of entering the public world. They are in dire need of maps—or of challenges to their existing sense of the terrain.

Popular culture, which is more and more taught at universities, generally cannot offer this. The objective of a good deal of rock music and film is to convey the pleasing illusion that people can live in the way that the singers and the actors comport themselves when they are on. Occasionally, I suppose, a performer comes through. Keith Richards seems to be, in life, the Keith that he evokes when he's onstage. Most people probably don't have the guts or the constitution for it.

Yet what David Denby says about movie love still strikes me as true: "Movie love puts people in touch with their own instincts and pleasures. Movies can lead to self-reconciliation, and that is one reason why they have inspired an almost unlimited affection." Movies tap into the fantasy life, and insofar as fantasy is being washed over by the gray waves of the reality principle, we need it to be restored. We need a new, larger self-synthesis that pays heed to the more refractory desires, or fantasies. But those fantasies cannot generally be the blueprint for a life, not in the way that the vision of Henry James, say, can conceivably be.

If resistance to popular culture is the teacher's objective, as it often is now, other problems arise. For the simple fact is that analysis will always be in arrears to the production of diverting images. While critique lingers over this or that blockbuster film, it becomes old news, the stuff of yesterday's generation. Brilliant analyses of *Titanic* are still coming out from learned journals and, in class, confronting students who were too young to have seen the film when it came out.

The central question to pose about works of popular culture, it seems to me, is this: Can you live it? Could you build a life around its visions? Given the work at hand, different people will answer differently. Some people will say yes to Bob Dylan (I would), yes to Muddy Waters and the blues tradition he works in, yes to Robert Altman or Stanley Kubrick. But you'll find far fewer people, I think, who'll be able to say yes to the Rolling Stones or Britney Spears. This doesn't mean that the Stones, and, who knows, maybe even Britney, are without their value. Fantasy matters. But I think that teaching such work to people who are looking for answers to primary questions may not be the best way to use their time.

Some humanities teachers, sometimes the best of them, feel that they're fighting in a lost if noble cause. They believe that the proliferation of electronic media will inevitably put them out of date. They see the time their students spend with TV and movies and on the Internet, and they feel that what they have to offer—words—must look shabby and old-fashioned by contrast. But this is not the case.

When human beings attempt to come to terms with who they are and who they wish to be, the most effective medium is verbal. Through words we represent ourselves to ourselves, we expand our awareness of the world, we step back, gain distance, on what it is we've said. And then we are in a position to change. Images, however exhilarating, do not generally function in this way. Words allow for a precision and nuance that images do not seem, for most people, to be able to provide. In a culture that changes at the velocity that ours does, the power of self-revision is centrally important. Self-aware self-revision is very difficult, if not impossible, outside of language.

Overall there is something to be learned from the analysis of popular culture. But we teachers can do better. We can strike to the central issues that confront the young, rather than working on the peripheries.

The other great apparent alternative to the self-creating approach I am describing goes under the name of multiculturalism. Know the other, says the multiculturalist. I could not agree more. A segment of the curriculum *should* be devoted to studying the literature and arts of cultures that are resolutely different from Western traditions. In them we may sometimes find truths that directly serve our present needs for revelation. We may read them and say: "Yes, that's how it is." But books from far-flung cultures can also teach us how many different ways of being there are in the world. In fact, this is probably their likeliest gift.

My fear about the multicultural curriculum is that it may ask students to know others before they know themselves. If we learn only or chiefly of difference without taking the time to find, or make, the inner being, we risk being walking voids, readily taken up by, say, commercial interests, ever ready to use our college-won knowledge of others for the purposes of exploiting them. Asks David Rieff: "Are the multiculturalists truly unaware of how closely their treasured catchphrases—'cultural diversity,' 'difference,' 'the need to do away with boundaries'—resemble the stock phrases of the modern corporation: 'product diversification,' 'the global marketplace,' and the 'boundary-less company'?" Where the inner void was, where the unbearable lightness was, there the corporation may well open its franchise.

Most of our ideas about influence are negative. Freud speaks of the transference, the influx of past memories that distort an existing erotic or power relation. Bloom writes of influence anxiety. And so the thought of being remade by the poets can cause people certain qualms. And yet perhaps the process I am describing is often not so much a matter of remaking or conversion as it is of recognition. T.S. Eliot observed that one of the things that poetry does is to find words for feelings that have abided unnamed in the heart. Maybe, on a larger scale, the process I am describing is simply one in which the self recognizes its own larger yet unarticulated order as it is shadowed forth in the thoughts of another. And then, of course, there is work to do, the work of completing the vision. As Nietzsche said, "No one can extract from things, books included, more than he already knows."

Proust, who is probably our preeminent theorist of a benevolent influence, observes that

> The mediocre usually imagine that to let ourselves be guided by the books we admire robs our faculty of judgment of part of its independence. "What can it matter to you what Ruskin feels: feel for yourself." Such a view rests on a psychological error which will be discounted by all who have accepted a spiritual discipline and feel thereby that their power of understanding and of feeling is infinitely enhanced and their critical sense never paralyzed . . . There is no better way of coming to be aware of what one feels oneself than by trying to recreate in oneself what a master has felt. In this profound effort it is our own thought itself that we bring out into the light together with his.

But the fact remains, as Proust elsewhere admits, that books can only put you on the edge of a spirited secular life. You must claim the rest, pass over the threshold for yourself.

Some will object to this vision of education. They will say that it is dangerous to talk about crucial matters in a classroom. A student's path may be radically changed by such discussion. The path may be blocked. It may become confused. But so may a life be ruined by not thinking. So may a life be ruined that never leaves the provinces of easy, unexamined faith in the transcendent. So may a life be wasted that gives to Falwell what he claims to be his and takes the slim remainder, worshipping diminutive Apollo with his toy computer, or small-time Dionysus with his Saturday nights. People can become distressed when they imagine a world in which all of us, inspired by poets and other artists, create our own lives, with only community welfare and our privately perceived failures to rein us in. They fear chaos, they say. They fear disorder. But perhaps what they fear, most truly, is democracy.

UNDER THE SIGN OF SATAN: BLAKE IN THE CORPORATE UNIVERSITY

> "I in my Selfhood am that Satan. I am that Evil One!"
>
> WILLIAM BLAKE, *MILTON*

IMAGINE WAKING UP in a world gone wrong. You can feel it: Things are out of joint. The center's not quite holding and all the rest. Yet imagine that world as being more agreeable— more secure, more organized, more civilized (in a certain sense)— than any world you had ever imagined inhabiting. One has a wealthy sponsor. One is sheltered, valued. There is the matter of prestige. There is a firm sense of identity, at the very least. One can do one's work. Distractions are few, privileges many. Yet still there is little doubt: One lives in a world gone wrong.

William Blake found himself in such a position when he turned himself over to the protection of his prosperous, kindly friend William Hayley. Hayley rescued Blake and his wife Catherine from poverty (maybe from financial ruin) and from the neglect that had plagued the poet-painter's work. Hayley brought Blake out of the blighted, glorious London that he loved and into the countryside. (Blake's attitude toward nature was complex, but overall unfavorable.) Haley gave Blake time, space, and money. He tried to make the poet into a success.

Blake's grand-sized visionary paintings didn't sell? No one wanted to buy his gorgeous, sometimes rather garishly illuminated books? Very well. Hayley wanted Blake to succeed. And Blake did not wish to be dependent on Hayley's charity forever. So Hayley put Blake to work painting miniatures, tiny portraits for broaches and necklaces. Blake, who loved to be expansive, was going to be compelled to do small things. But Hayley loved Blake—Blake knew it. He truly wanted this man of genius to prosper, gain recognition, stand on his feet and all the rest. In a sense, Blake never had a better friend than William Hayley.

2

No one liked it when Hulk Hogan came to town. At least no one I know did. Hulk came to Charlottesville to perform with his wrestling troupe at the John Paul Jones Arena at the University of Virginia. We had imagined, my faculty friends and I, that the arena would be the site for UVA basketball games and maybe a graduation ceremony or two on rainy days. But not long after the grand opening of the arena, we heard about Hulk and his crew, and we heard of a performance by something called monster trucks. The climax, I understood, came when a particularly monstrous monster truck, with tires taller than two or three men, rode over the tops of a line of parked vehicles, crushing them into metal pulp.

When the subject of Hulk Hogan and the monster trucks arose, my faculty buddies and I *looked* at each other in exasperated ways and blew out exasperated columns of air as if to scatter the wrestlers and the steroidal trucks like so many leaves. But we did not *say* all that much. No, not much at all.

The University of Virginia, like virtually all universities, is a corporation. It requires revenues. It needs to generate funds. There is an operating budget and expenses must be met, among them the expenses of maintaining me in the English department, and my friends in music and architecture and religious studies.

That universities are becoming more corporate in orientation and aim is news to no one at all. We—like every other school that aspires to a certain status, a certain measure of success—have added layer upon layer of administrators. We have brought on no end of fund-raisers. More than that, many of the deans once charged with overseeing academic affairs are now also out seeking money from donors. A story that appeared not terribly long ago in the *New York Times* tells us that over the past two decades, colleges and universities in America have doubled their full-time support staff. Enrollment has increased only 40 percent; full-time instructors rose by only 50 percent, and many of those new instructors are non–tenure track. The article goes on to say that "the growth in support staff included some jobs that did not exist 20 years ago, like environmental sustainability officers and a broad array of information technology workers. The support staff category includes many different jobs, like residential-life staff, admissions and recruitment officers, fund-raisers, loan counselors and all the back-office staff positions responsible for complying with the new regulations and reporting requirements college faces."

With these changes, a new institutional culture is coming into being. Universities now teem with people who must do what people who work in corporations do: be responsive to their superiors, direct their underlings, romance their BlackBerries, subordinate their identities, refrain from making mistakes, keep a gimlet eye always on the bottom line. Organization men and women have come and they are doing what they can—for an administrator must administer something—to influence the shape of the university. Are they having a shaping influence on the students? Often they do not have to, for many of our students—not all, but many—are already organization men and women. Though "organization man" is not the name in favor now; the current term of art is "leader."

How does a young person begin to qualify to become what is now called a leader? The essayist William Deresiewicz talks about the endless series of hoops that students have to jump through now if they hope to get into the right colleges. "Courses, standardized tests, extra-curriculars in school, extra-curriculars outside school. Test prep courses, admissions coaches, private tutors." What you get at the end, he says, are "kids who have been trained to be excellent hoop jumpers." They are, as one member of the generation observes, "excellent sheep."

All colleges and universities want leaders. They want to recruit them from high school. They want to cultivate them once they've arrived. Colleges are determined to graduate leaders and to send them into the world to become prosperous and grateful alumni. But who is a leader? A leader is someone who is drawn to organizations. He learns their usages. He internalizes their rules. He merges his identity with that of the organization. He always says "we." He starts at the bottom, a leader in training. Then he progresses, always by gradual steps, as close to the top as his powers will allow. He begins "mentoring" other leaders. In his assent, he is assiduous to get along with people. He blends in like a white moth on a whitewashed picked fence. Everyone likes him. He gives no offense and where possible he takes none. He questions the presiding powers but in the manner of a minor angel, inquiring into the ways of his more opulently fledged brethren.

3

In "London," perhaps his best-known poem, Blake takes on the role of the biblical prophet—Isaiah, Ezekiel, Jeremiah—and rambles through the great city. What he sees stuns him. He is sick to articulate rage about it. The human aspirations to kindliness, community, and gentleness have been drowned in hypocrisy. The little chimney sweep's cry "every black'ning church appalls." The sweeps, orphaned, sold into something tantamount to slavery, get no succor from the church. Their cries blacken an already black, hulking monolith. The soldier's sigh "runs in blood down palace walls." Wars far away—in America, among other places—have sent soldiers off to risk their lives, not for noble ends but to suppress liberty and open up new markets for British merchants.

But perhaps worst of all in Blake's London is the state of love. (Blake greatly values heterosexual love—is in love with it.) The wandering prophet, edging toward rage, about to go over to Rintrah, as Blake liked to put it, hears "how the youthful harlot's curse / Blasts the newborn infant's tear / And blights with plagues the marriage hearse." Prostitution—sex for money—is to Blake one of the worst human depravities. The man of property, subject to an arranged marriage, flies to the prostitute. She gives him an escape from his loveless marriage; she gives him some measure of intrigue and excitement. She also gives him syphilis, which ruins the marriage and infects his child and wife.

The church should engender a community of loving-kindness. The army should encourage bravery in just wars. Lovers should meet and love regardless of finances and social class. Sexual joy should be the culmination of real attraction of body and mind, whether sanctified by marriage or not. Prophets should not be compelled to rage blindly through the streets of London, witnesses to human despair. "I mark," says Blake, "in every face I meet / Marks of weakness, marks of woe." The prophet should offer wise and genial counsel and not be compelled to tremble with rage.

4

The engineering student sits in the fiction writer's office and asks questions about her craft. This fiction thing, this art thing, what is it about? What is it about *exactly*? He has read some novels. He plans to read many more. His grade-point average is high. His SAT scores are also impressive. A nearly perfect score on the verbals: He makes sure to mention this. He is—he knows—very smart.

But this fiction thing and poetry as well. How does one begin? (The fellow who wrote *Crying of Lot 49*—what was his name?— he was an engineering student, no?) There are, one hears, guide books, which give step-by-step instructions. Does the teacher advise trying one?

The teacher's way of writing fiction is to find an image, something that lodged in her mind for no reason that she can understand. She writes the image down. She describes it as well as she can from a vantage point that is—maybe—not quite her own.

And then what? The student is truly interested.

She waits then to see what will happen from there.

And?

Sometimes something happens. Sometimes nothing.

This is writing? This is what you do?

Other people do it differently. But yes. I wait to see what will happen. She tells the students that if she lets her attention float with just the right amount of freedom, she'll eventually go somewhere she's fascinated by going.

Why don't you just start with what fascinates you?

I don't always know, the writer confesses. I don't always really know.

5

Satan weeps frequently. It is surprising, but it is true. In Blake's epic, *Milton,* Satan is a cultivated, thoughtful, highly sensitive specimen of what the eighteenth century liked to call a Man of Sensibility. He is not overwhelmingly intellectual. He appears to put feelings before thoughts. Nor is he the fiery, rather charismatic figure that Milton conjures up with a massive more-than-Achillean shield and a spear to which the tallest Norwegian pine tree is but a wand. Blake's Satan has no tail, no claws, no fangs, no cloven foot, not even an odor of pitch on arrival and departure. This Satan is urbanely kind. He is Hayley, the man who brought Blake out of London to Felpham, so Blake the genius might be saved. Of course there are the miniatures, which Blake does not wish to paint. "When Hayley finds out what you cannot do / That is the very thing he'll set you to," Blake complains. There are also some tensions in sensibility: Hayley, who is Satan, is rather on the refined side. "Hayley on his toilette seeing the soap / Cries, 'Homer is very much improv'd by Pope.'" Hayley prefers Pope's refined translations of *The Iliad* and *The Odyssey* to Homer's actual unflinching vision. Being on the toilet close to his odorous humanity makes Hayley long for purity, long for Pope.

Hayley—and Satan, too—love poetry. They are drawn to poets; they find them mysterious, alluring, perhaps rather enviable. But then comes the question: Why should they, Satan and Hayley, not be poets as well? Already they have succeeded brilliantly at what they've set their hands to do. Hayley is good at business, better than good. As to Satan—here matters get more complicated. Satan has a cosmic role: He presides over time, clock time, ordering, duration. He is the lord of Chrons. All forms of regulation, consistency, and order fall under his power. He grinds time the way a farmer grinds wheat. No sand grain passes through the glass of time without Satan's awareness and approval. He propels the sun punctually through the houses of the zodiac. He measures the shadows on the moon's white face. He is God as a watchmaker, God as a supreme engineer.

But this is not enough for him. Satan also wants to be a poet. He is infatuated with Palamabron, the giant figure who wields the harrow. Palamabron breaks in order to create again; he engraves the soil; his work is sustenance to those who hunger in spirit as well as body. Palamabron concentrates all that Blake feels to be true about true artists. An idealization? Yes, maybe. But Blake deals in giant forms—grand, emblematic concentrations of force.

Finally Satan prevails upon Los, father of the eternals, to let him take Palamabron's harrow from his hands. What happens then? "Satan labour'd all day—it was a thousand years." Or at least it probably felt that way to Blake—the age of Pope and Dryden and Joshua Reynolds and Locke and Hobbes is a desert of tedium to Blake. It probably feels like a millennium. Engineers, people who wanted to understand art, draw blueprints, then get to work constructing things, were now the lords of light who lived where true thinkers and artists should have resided. A mess!

The mess has a double dimension, though. Palamabron's poetic attendants—Blake calls then gnomes—take over Satan's time-grinding mills. They get drunk as a tribe of monkeys and stumble around singing the songs of Palamabron. Minutes presumably last hours now; sometimes seconds probably expand into days; some days go blink and are gone. Another mess! The gnomes want to get back to the field, start engraving, start creating again—though getting drunk and messing with temporality is probably diverting to them for a little while.

Satan always wants to grasp the harrow—he wants to be lord high commissioner of everything and creator spirit, all at the same time. He wants to dominate time—as the bureaucrat of the minute—and also to live outside of time where real creation takes place. He wants to engineer odes.

Sometimes Blake loses all of his patience with Satan and wants to purge him out and away. Get thee behind me, and all of that. In *Milton* there is a culminating scene in which Blake, possessed by an apocalyptic fury, goes on about being washed clean in the blood of the lamb and purging away all of the nonhuman until "Generation is swallowed up in Regeneration," nature is swallowed up by true human culture. No more Satan then, no more crippling dualisms, just the bliss of ongoing creation, which Blake calls Eden.

6

Yet at other times one feels that Blake rather likes Satan, much as he rather liked Hayley. "Corporeal friends are spiritual enemies," Blake famously said. Yes, perhaps. But perhaps only to the measure that artists, spiritual questers, allow them to be. Palamabron could presumably have told Los—the executive faculty of the mind, the spirit of the age, whatever he might be—to Take Off when he demanded the plough for Satan. Artists need Satan to run the world. There must be surgeons and airline pilots and directors of academic fund-raising. Satan is, after all, "Prince of the Starry Hosts / And of the Wheels of Heaven," and in this there is some honor—as long as Satan retains his place and stays off Palamabron's rightful turf.

Artists need a Satanic side sometimes, too. You've got to know how to butter your parsnips, Frost said. ("Provide! Provide!" He cries out to his old crone who was once a star of the silver screen and is now scouring the front steps "with pail and rag.") Satan often knows where the butter dish is stored.

It can be tempting for the artist to give up and to hand everything over to Satan. Or to be too compliant when Satan asks: Are there books with blueprints for how to write a poem? Of course there are, the weary and neglected writer replies. Good ones, too. She resolves that tonight maybe she'll have a peek.

The contemporary artist can be prone to forget what he stands for in a way that Blake never did. Or he can get weary, as Blake surely did, of endorsing his ideals in a culture that cares little for them. Blake knew what he wanted: love that exalted lover and beloved; he knew that the measure of a society is the care, affection, and wisdom that it expends on children. Blake disliked war. He preferred what he called "mental fight." But he surely preferred just wars, like the American Revolution, which gladdened and amazed him, to unjust ones. He wanted poets to be prophets and call things as they saw them. He told us these things in "London." He seems to have meant them. He left his giant forms to remind us.

Hulk Hogan and those monster trucks are giant forms in their own ways. They are, I suppose, Satan's idea of poetry at its very worst: obvious, noisy, and lucrative. They're such gross caricatures that in time even Satan is probably made weary of them. He would dearly love it, I half believe, if Palamabron in his current form would take the harrow out of his hands and if he would tell Hulk, who seems as amiable as Hayley, that it is time to go home. But the contemporary Palamabron has experienced deconstruction and pragmatism and cultural studies and he knows how to see the world with what Nietzsche called a "perspectival seeing." He doubts his every reflex, Palamabron does. He cannot love what he loves. He cannot believe in eternal truth or everlasting beauty. So now he abides Satan, who in his heart probably does not want to be tolerated half so well.

For why did the administrators who are coming more and more to dominate the academic scene come to academia in the first place? Why didn't they stay in business where the salaries are higher, the perks cushier, and where everyone seems to receive weekly and free of charge a zippy new handheld wireless device? Maybe they came because they wanted to learn things—enduring things, humane things. They wanted to be in a place where people talked about Plato and Blake and Shakespeare and Schopenhauer, rather than exclusively about Hulk Hogan and the bottom line. I sometimes think that there are more *potential* intellectual idealists among the administrators than among the faculty. But as long as we professors can't tell them exactly what's wrong with Hulk Hogan and the monster trucks, what are they supposed to do? As long as we can't say why Shakespeare is better than the next episode of *Jersey Shore*, how will they help us and help universities to be enduring centers of learning and of art?

If you don't cultivate (and discipline) Satan, he'll grow ever more powerful and ever more pragmatic. He'll come to represent worldly values and nothing else and his confidence in these values will grow and grow. So when Satan in his current guise finally tells Palamabron to fall down and worship him, what will—what can?—Palamabron do?

A NOTE ON THE AUTHOR

Mark Edmundson teaches at the University of Virginia, where he is University Professor. A prizewinning scholar, he is also the author of *Why Read?*, *Teacher*, *The Death of Sigmund Freud*, and *The Fine Wisdom and Perfect Teachings of the Kings of Rock and Roll*. His writing has appeared in such publications as the *New Republic*, the *New York Times Magazine*, the *Nation*, and *Harper's*. He lives in Batesville, Virginia.